Considering
A New Call
ethical and spiritual
challenges for clergy

JAMES M. ANTAL
FOREWORD BY JOHN H. THOMAS

An Alban Institute Publication

Copyright © 2000 by the Alban Institute. All rights reserved.

This material may not be photocopied or reproduced in any way without written permission.

Library of Congress Catalog Card Number 99-69587

ISBN 1-56699-231-1

IN MEMORY OF MY FATHER

JERRY ANTAL

1916–1995

TABLE OF CONTENTS

FOREWORD

A lay leader once asked me, with tongue not quite in cheek, "Why is it that God always seems to call ministers to larger churches offering bigger salaries?" Of course, this is not always the case, but there is enough truth behind this gentle barb to make most ministers uncomfortable. For beyond the lofty language of "call" and "spiritual discernment," most of us who are ordained know that other factors always intrude into the process discussed in this book. Career advancement, financial needs, status among colleagues, location, a spouse's employment opportunities, and a child's educational needs all play strong roles in the consideration of a new call. A brief glance at the "opportunities" section of religious journals such as *The Christian Century* reveals the extent to which discernment of call is influenced by the consumer mentality of the secular marketplace. Is it any wonder that a profession annually identifying itself as "self-employed" for the IRS becomes confused and vaguely embarrassed by the seeming contradiction between the church's lofty language of call and the culture's expectation about career? Nowhere is this ambivalence felt more strongly than when a minister considers a new call.

I remember toward the end of my first pastorate as an associate in a large suburban parish, a tenure marked by a high degree of enjoyment and satisfaction, wrestling with the questions, Should I stay? Should I go? My wise senior colleague, sensing my restlessness, helped press the question.

"I guess I always thought something new and compelling would simply fall into my lap and it would become obvious that it was time to move," I said.

"Perhaps that does happen sometimes," he replied, "but you may also need to move your lap around a little."

Jim Antal's book combines this kind of concrete, down-to-earth advice with a profound theological and moral reflection on the ambiguities inherent for pastors and people in the search process. Drawing on rich biblical imagery as well as the theological traditions of the church, Antal probes the challenging dilemmas facing ministers seeking to be faithful to the demands of their current call while remaining attentive to the Spirit's prompting that may signal the need to discern a new call. He faces the tough realities of how confidentiality may require deception, how servant leadership and personal or family needs intersect or collide, how saying "good-bye" to the old and "hello" to the new may lead to unexpected and occasionally painful reactions. He acknowledges both grief and gratitude, and calls upon all of us to respond with grace. Throughout the book Antal writes as a pastor "who has been there." Thus, his words ring true and his advice bears the integrity of theological reflection rooted in the reality of pastoral experience.

While ministers considering a new call will be the obvious primary audience for this book, at least two other groups will profit from reading it as well. The first includes members of search committees in local churches who, in most cases, will have little or no experience preparing them for the critical task they are undertaking. In a few cases, these search committee members may have been selected by their congregations because they work in human resources or personnel. For either person, the search process for a new minister will be a bewildering experience requiring gifts never before exercised or challenging secular assumptions about how to hire a new employee. This book legitimates the realities of both types of committee members and can help them maneuver through the moral and spiritual uncertainties that don't belong to the minister alone. Furthermore, discovering the tension ministers feel between call and career will invite these lay leaders to deeper reflection about the meaning of their own careers, that is, their own careers may also be a "calling" offering opportunities for ministry and requiring their own moral and spiritual discernment.

The larger audience, of course, is the church itself. Antal's book brings into focus much of the confusion and uncertainty that exists today, at least among Protestants, over the meaning of ministry and the significance of ordination. To whom does the ministry of the church belong? Is ministry a function, something we take up or set aside at will? Or does ordination to ministry endow us with a particular quality or character that sets ministers apart in some essential way? If God's calling is always embodied, made incarnate, in what ways can the culture, and in particular secular management and employment expertise, teach us to be more faithful and effective in ministry, and when must we resist cultural norms in order to be faithful? When is a job also a calling? A creative use of this book would be for pastor and people to read and discuss this book together when it is clear that the pastor is clearly *not* currently considering a new call. Such a reading could lead to a fascinating exploration of the joys and struggles of ministry for both clergy and laity, and could address much confusion that often leads to heartbreak and to decisions to leave before "it's time."

Finally, Antal reminds those of us who are ministers of the critical importance of *collegial* discernment. Throughout these pages, the value of trusted colleagues to whom we can turn for counsel, wisdom, and encouragement is evident. Judicatory executives, denominational colleagues, and ecumenical friends can all be critical companions in considering a new call. Lone rangers are vulnerable to many perils in ministry, and the process of discerning a new call is no exception. As one of our colleagues, Antal has given us a thoughtful, reasoned, and articulate voice. All of us who must struggle with the demands, delights, and seductions of our calling will welcome his insights and be grateful for his labor.

JOHN H. THOMAS
General Minister and President
United Church of Christ

Not long after beginning this project, I attended an Alban Institute conference entitled "Leading the Large Church." More than 40 newly called senior ministers of large churches from various denominations gathered to hear Ed White, senior consultant of the Alban Institute, and John M. Buchanan, senior pastor of Fourth Presbyterian Church in Chicago (subsequently elected moderator of the 208th General Assembly of the Presbyterian Church U.S.A.). I had been busy hammering out notes on my laptop computer throughout the conference, and I told my colleagues that I would be glad to send them each a copy of the notes. They responded with grateful applause. Then I mentioned that I was in the early stages of writing this book. In return for my notes, I invited them to send me stories of their experiences while searching for a new ministerial position.

Obviously the topic touched a nerve. Almost immediately, a few colleagues called out, "Oh, do I have a story for you!" and "I can't wait to tell you!" I heard the same enthusiasm every time I mentioned this topic to a colleague. I discovered that not only did everyone have a story—and often many stories!—to tell, but most of them were deeply grateful to be asked.

We ministers don't often talk about our searches, mostly out of concern for confidentiality and sometimes out of fear that we may be competing for the same spot. We don't talk with parishioners because most searches are carried out without the minister's current congregation knowing. We don't talk with friends because the risk that something we say could get back to the congregation is not worth taking. We don't talk with our denominational representative because he or she is often busy and has likely heard it all before.

Yet, amidst this isolation, we find ourselves facing some of the more complicated ethical and spiritual challenges of our lives. If we are married, we may share our struggles with our spouse (rarely with our children), but for the most part we must assess which path we will take, and discern where God would have us go, without the benefit of the views of the community to which we have given our lives.

When we initiate a search for a new church, we would do well to reflect on the meaning of Jesus' observation in the Sermon on the Mount: "No one can serve two masters; for a slave will either hate the one and love the other, or be devoted to the one and despise the other. You cannot serve God and wealth" (Matt. 6:24). This passage makes clear that there are some loyalties which cannot be divided or subordinated. Our commitment to God must remain our primary loyalty. If it is subordinated to any other commitment, such as the pursuit of wealth or ambition or pleasure, then we can no longer legitimately claim discipleship.

When a minister initiates a search for a new church, his or her loyalties are inevitably divided in a variety of ways. Some of these conflicts resemble the "two masters" passage. We often find our faithfulness to God pitted against our worldly desires. In addition, a fundamental conflict arises when God appears to call us to serve in two mutually exclusive settings, that is, our current churches as well as a possible future church. Knowing what is required of us under these conditions is challenging, to say the least!

Occasionally the search process requires us to make a choice not unlike Jesus' reference to the dichotomy between God and wealth. Almost always, a search raises serious questions about the authenticity of our current ministries as well as our own integrity, questions not unrelated to the broad, ethical investigation Jesus undertakes in the Sermon on the Mount.

Of the myriad ways that initiating the search process divides our loyalties, three are worth mentioning in detail. The first involves a conflict between service to God and service to our present congregations. Under normal conditions, most ministers with whom I have spoken are not saddled with anxiety about the authenticity of their current calls. But once a minister senses that God may be calling him or her elsewhere, suddenly two haunting questions are introduced: Can I be authentic in my current ministry? Is this potential position truly a call from God or is it merely a temptation?

If it were possible for us to be blessed with certainty from the moment we discerned a new direction, this particular tension would be resolved. But the process of discernment is undertaken over time. While we may hope that some human form of certainty may eventually result, we must wait for it to unfold. Thus, from the moment we open ourselves to the possibility of an alternative call, we serve two masters: the continuing sense that we are called to advance God's purposes in our current setting, and the sense that we must attend to the new thing God may be calling us to explore.

The second way in which our loyalties are divided is rooted in the tension between vocation and ambition. The root of the word *vocation* is the Latin *vocare*, which means "to call." But for us, the emphasis is on the source of the call: It comes from outside ourselves and draws us in a particular direction—occasionally, as suggested in John 21:18, to a place we would rather not go. To understand our vocation, we must look beyond ourselves to the source of the call. Robert Schnase, minister and author, defines ambition as "the ardent desire to high position or to attain rank, influence, distinction."[1] Ambition originates in the self. To understand its force and direction, it is necessary to look inward.

Upon initiating the search process, we find ourselves caught up in an awkward tension. Are we considering a new direction because God is calling us from outside of ourselves, or are we pushing ourselves to investigate new possibilities? I do not want to reduce the importance of ambition in ministers' lives. Its presence can enormously enhance the quality of one's ministry.[2] But those who ignore the resulting tension between ambition and vocation do so at their own peril. Indeed, these alternative motivations can represent two masters. Only when we are clear about our motivations can we truly devote ourselves to serving God and making our lives a transparent window to God's life so that, through us, our congregants might gain a better understanding of God.

Finally, there is a third way our loyalties are divided soon after we initiate a search. As anyone who has looked for a job knows, searching for a new job is a full-time activity. Search committees receive scores of profiles, and the quality of those profiles determines whom they pursue. Achieving that quality takes time. Tension results when one considers that each hour put into revising and updating a profile is an hour not spent in pastoral counseling, sermon preparation, or some other activity that would benefit our current congregations. This tension is not limited to clergy, of course. But the issue of loyalty is so closely linked to service that when we ministers "go a courting" to another congregation, not only do we feel disloyal, many of us feel as though we are betraying our current congregations.

My reason for writing this book has everything to do with these three tensions. The ingredients of these tensions form the foundation to our understanding and fulfillment of our ministries. Most ministers are not accustomed to the imbalance experienced when a search is initiated. And, when we feel off balance, our decisions often leave much to be desired.

By bringing together the reflections of many clergy with whom I have discussed these questions, I hope to provide ministers with a light along the dark alley of answering a new call. Some of that light is provided by the text, and some is found in the footnotes and citations on the pages that follow. Together they offer a rigorous review of the relatively few resources that focus on the search process from the point of view of clergy. The rest of that light is found in identifying and examining the ethical dilemmas and spiritual conundrums occasioned by a search. Knowing in advance some of the challenges that lie ahead can only add intentionality and integrity to a process that demands both, even while it threatens to compromise them.

A key ingredient for any minister engaged in a search is his or her immediate family. Drawing wisdom and perspective from our most intimate relationships and sharing mutually in the many decisions along the way are crucial to the process. Although ministers' families span the full spectrum of relationships (including single, married, straight, gay, with or without biological and/or adopted children), in a few sections of this book I focus on dynamics likely to be present in straight, married relationships, perhaps including children. The bulk of my interviews were with ministers in these types of relationships. Nevertheless, further study is needed to address the unique dynamics of other types of relationships.

The approach I have taken in this book is informed and guided by the ethics training I received from professors who were particularly influenced by Protestant theologian H. Richard Niebuhr.[3] Although I have made no formal attempt to draw directly from his works, the development of the themes of character, freedom, destiny, and responsibility—all of which are taken up in H. Richard Niebuhr's writings[4]—are central to this analysis.

By the time we reached seminary, most of us realized that the notion of calling was both mysterious and complex. But after being settled for a while in a church, when we begin to experience a curiosity or an attraction toward another position, or perhaps God doing a "new thing" (Rev. 21:5) in us, we can readily become mired in the mystery and complexity of our vocation. I hope that these pages will unpack the complexity without reducing the mystery, and thus maintain our connection with the One who called us and calls us still.

ACKNOWLEDGMENTS

I arrived at the Newton Highlands Congregational Church in 1986 with much to learn. The wonderful people of that congregation taught me a great deal about love and helped me to become a more effective parish minister. Among them were numerous faculty and administrators of Andover Newton Theological School, with whom I shared much and from whom I learned a great deal. Their persistent encouragement motivated me to enroll in the doctorate of ministry (D.Min.) program and complete the thesis on which this book is based.

Jerry Handspicker, Mary Luti, and my rabbi friend, David Whiman, offered much appreciated support and friendship. The encouragement of my wife, Cindy Shannon, has been unflinching. Her suggestions and insights, not to mention her partnership in several searches, have made this a much better book. The enthusiasm of the ministers I have spoken to has buoyed me up when my own momentum slowed. Their honesty has provided much of the substance of this book. Where the case studies are undeveloped or the ideas insufficiently explored, the responsibility is mine alone.

The path that led to my current parish was paved with many lessons. Some are in these pages. What must be added here is the gratitude I feel for those faithful and loving members of my past and present congregations, Newton Highlands Congregational Church and Plymouth Church of Shaker Heights, who have supported and challenged me as we listened for God's call. Without the lessons they have taught me these pages could not have been written.

INTRODUCTION

Regardless of our denominational affiliation, as clergy involved in a search process, we face a common set of dilemmas that arise out of distinctive features of parish ministry. Consider this sampling of circumstances. We are bound to our current congregations through a covenant, which the initiation of a search will undermine. We are called to our current congregations by the Holy Spirit, which will need to blow in a new direction if we are to initiate a search. We live among our current congregations as public figures, which will be compromised if we undertake a private search for a new call. And, we are trusted by our current congregants. Keeping a search secret will invite suspicion and arouse distrust, thus undermining our current ministries.

As ministers, priests, and rabbis, we all wrestle with concerns that arise from a shift in the delicate balance between fidelity to God's call, fidelity to our current congregation, and our understanding of new possibilities God places before us. Such a shift can be seismic or subtle. It can push us to have a conversation with the bishop or to request the forms we need to complete our resumes or profiles.[1]

Regardless of the differences in polity among various denominations[2]—and they are considerable—clergy of all stripes will find the issues examined in this book both familiar and without sufficient discussion in most professional settings.[3] In addition to exploring many of the unexamined issues that all clergy face, these pages offer some practical illustrations. These illustrations tend to concentrate on those denominational settings that allow both candidates and congregations autonomy in circulating clergy and church profiles. Clergy of other denominations will benefit from the broader theological, spiritual, and ethical reflections found in these pages.

While this book focuses on distinct challenges faced by clergy as they undertake a search, it's worth noting at the outset that many of the reasons for initiating a search are similar to the motivations that drive professionals in the workforce to change positions. In my conversations with numerous clergy,[4] the following reasons have been cited: lack of ongoing challenge, sense of having mastered one's current position, interest in a different form of ministry or different type of staff position, ambition, spouse's desire to move, salary, health care options, conflict in present congregation, sense of better opportunity elsewhere.

Clergy also have much in common with their lay colleagues in undertaking the search process itself. To begin, looking for a new job usually involves a lot of hard work. The process is emotionally, mentally, and physically draining. In fact, looking for a new job registers among the three most stressful life events. The search process inevitably involves a sobering look inward, even as it demands much outward investigation. Those of us who look for new employment soon discover that our marketability is not solely related to the quality of our current work. Other factors, many of which we cannot control, enter the equation. Finding a new position involves considering compatibility on an almost endless number of fronts, including both professional and personal criteria. Invariably, the culmination of the process involves negotiation, a process few do well.

The search process itself is similar to the process engaged by our lay colleagues. According to a United Church of Christ (U.C.C.) minister, who is now retired, informal discussions between the conference minister, the outgoing senior minister, and the search committee (sometimes known as the "old boy network") have been known to play a critical role in some searches. Based on such discussions, a search committee would simply invite the identified candidate for a visit, including an interview and an opportunity to preach. Because the polity of the U.C.C. guarantees congregational autonomy, such an approach was possible in the past. This autonomy, enjoyed by individual congregations and guaranteed by the polity of the U.C.C., allows congregations to follow their own lights.

Some so-called searches comprise merely verbal recommendations from former senior ministers. This retired U.C.C. minister knew of one conference minister who was responsible for arranging appointments between churches and candidates and would frequently interject a trusted, authoritative word in favor of one candidate over the rest, thus exerting substantial influence on the committee. While there is enormous variation between conferences and associations, and even regions, remnants of this sort of approach are readily found today as churches look for new leadership.

We who find ourselves considering a new setting discover that we must contend with a number of challenges few others face, the most obvious of which is often ignored. The life of a parish minister is inevitably public. Our activities—in restaurants, at our children's sporting events, in the grocery store, at the hairdresser, driving the car—are noticed and talked about.

Edwin Friedman makes this point with a joke. Comparing the relationship clergy have with their congregations to the relationship psychiatrists have with their patients, he asks, "What if, as a psychiatrist, all of your patients got together in your office once a week and talked about you—that is, you and your family? And what if they assembled every year and, after dismissing you from the room, then set your fees after comparing their various encounters with you?" This process, although obviously absurd for a psychiatrist, is typical of what clergy experience. Although some clergy enjoy being in the public eye, none covet a congregation talking behind their backs. Thus, clergy seek ways to preserve a modicum of privacy, for themselves and for their families. Among other strategies, many clergy maintain out-of-state friendships, limit socializing, and closely monitor what they say about their spouses or children.

Yet, the farther clergy proceed in the search process, attempts to maintain privacy are at best extremely awkward, at worst failed. Whether or not individual ministers seek privacy in their personal affairs, the vast majority engage the search process with every intention of keeping it to themselves. But, since most churches are small, congregations are often places where members know everyone's business. This is in sharp contrast to a typical secular work environment, which tends to be more segmented and enables discretion more easily. When clergy look at a possible new church, their current congregations may discover this new development in any number of ways. Some stem from breaches of confidentiality at the prospective church, others occur from happenstance that simply cannot be anticipated or controlled.

An example is a ministerial candidate at a church on the West Coast, 3,000 miles from his present congregation. The neutral pulpit at which he preached was in a different city, another 40 miles away. While greeting the congregation following the service, an older couple stepped forward in the line. They were on vacation, visiting from Maine, and had just happened to come to worship that Sunday at the local church. They were the parents of a woman belonging to the minister's Boston congregation. In fact, the minister remembered meeting them at the wedding ceremony between their daughter and another member of his church. While coincidences like this can happen to anyone, in any profession, the conundrums they cause for clergy can severely affect a minister's current and future ministry.

Another aspect peculiar to a ministry search is the minister's capacity to lead worship and preach. It is a crucial quality any church must investigate in a candidate, but the opportunity to see a candidate in action occurs only on Sunday morning. Thus, for direct evaluation to take place, the committee must observe the candidate either in his or her current congregation, or in a neutral pulpit. Rarely do search committees' church visits go undetected. Never do congregants fail to notice a Sunday when their pastor is absent. In no other profession are the opportunities for review by a prospective employer so restricted. And in no other profession are prospective employers so resistant to a candidate's discretion.

Finally, once a church realizes its need for a new pastor, the search is invariably a lengthy process, taking from nine months to more than two years. Once a candidate has been contacted, completing the process can still take anywhere from two months to two years. The longer the process, the greater the likelihood that confidentiality will be compromised.

The risk of compromising confidentiality intensifies in the final stage of the search, once the committee has extended an offer and the candidate has accepted. From that moment on, the search committee wants to do whatever it can to promote and "sell" its choice to the congregation. This usually involves publishing a biographical sketch of the candidate, along with a description of the process that led to the committee's decision. Even if this is done with the utmost discretion and care, church members who have been awaiting this announcement will be eager to talk about their much-anticipated new minister. Many will ponder whether or not they know someone who knows the new pastor, or knows someone in his or her congregation. Enthusiasm propels investigative phone calls and e-mails, and before you know it, members of the minister's current congregation discover that their minister is about to leave them for another church and that they are the last ones to hear about it!

With the advent of electronic communication (particularly Web sites), a new medium by which this announcement can be communicated is available. The only problem is that if the announcement is made available on the Internet, it becomes available to everyone—including anyone from the minister's current congregation.

Is all of this so bad? While anyone presently holding a job who goes in search of a new one discovers that some form of deceit in one's present workplace is almost inevitable, ministers who deceive may jeopardize their current and future job and their own sense of integrity. If seminarians were given advance warning that a call from God to move on would almost certainly, at some level, mean deceiving their current congregations, their responses would likely be something less than positive. For pastoral ministerial leadership to be effective, it must have integrity. Breach the integrity and you impair the ministry.

This points to my reason for writing this book. I believe that clergy who reflect upon some of the seemingly impossible (but true!) circumstances that illustrate these pages will be better prepared to preserve their integrity in the face of any number of powerful challenges. Of the clergy with whom I have talked, many have said they were surprised again and again in their processes. These surprises have often involved ethical dilemmas or spiritual conundrums and have sapped them of much of their energy. As noted earlier, because we ministers typically do not talk with one another about our search experiences, each of us is in the dark about what we might expect.

I hope this book can shine even a dim light on the path of those who read it. Perhaps you, the reader, will be able to be more intentional about your decisions and more obedient and prayerful about God's call in your daily life. Perhaps this book will help you shorten the search process, which is often extended when clergy feel trapped by ethical dilemmas or find themselves slumped in a spiritual conundrum, and thus devote more time to serving God's children, whether they live in your current congregation or your next one.

First Things First: Thou Shalt Have No Other Gods Before Me

Take delight in the Lord, and he will give you the desires of your heart.

Psalms 37:4

When Bob Dylan became interested in Christianity, he wrote one of the first Christian rock songs to gain widespread attention, *Gotta Serve Somebody*.[1] As is typical of a newcomer in the faith, Dylan casts the choice of whom one might serve in rather stark terms: "It might be the Devil, or it might be the Lord, but you're gonna have to serve somebody."

Most clergy are clear about the fact that ministry involves service but are remarkably imprecise when pressed with the question, Exactly whom or what are you serving? Numerous alternatives abound beyond the two Dylan mentions. For example, clergy are also called to serve their present congregations. Clergy must also pay attention to—and in some sense serve— their unfulfilled ambitions, both within and beyond ministry. And clergy with life partners must consider the consequences of being in a lifelong relationship that may include the lives and futures of children.

Perhaps it is no surprise that a popular book entirely focused on the clergy search process devotes less than a page to this question.[2] In three years of interviewing candidates for ministry as a member of the Committee on Ministry of the Metropolitan Boston Association of the Massachusetts Conference of the United Church of Christ, I cannot recall hearing a candidate address the issue of call in any but vague, self-authenticating ways. Without referring directly to the notion of call, author Loren Mead notes that the entire process of initiating a search usually comes as a surprise, not only to the congregation (when they find out) but even to the clergy person.[3] Without a doubt, clergy could benefit from a better understanding of the subtle and complex dynamics of call in their lives.

Wm. Bud Phillips offers perhaps the most nuanced assessment of the psychological aspects involved in clergy transitions. He begins his book Pastoral Transitions noting, "No one ever really knows when endings begin. . . ." and continues with chapters on disenchantment, dis-identification, disorganization, and disengagement.[4] While this analysis is enormously interesting, it is based on the fundamental assumption that clergy initiate transitions because something negative or unsatisfying prompts them to move on. My conversations with clergy echo the truth of his assumption in many—perhaps most—cases. What is sometimes difficult to acknowledge, and always difficult to discern, is whether those negative or unsatisfying experiences might also be signals from God and vehicles of call.

William Sloane Coffin Jr. offers an engaging assessment of the distinction between career and calling.[5] Noting that the words car and career both come from carrera, the Latin word for "racetrack," Coffin emphasizes that the questions associated with pursuing a career are entirely different from those raised when considering a calling.

> A career seeks to be successful, a calling to be valuable. A career tries to make money, a calling tries to make a difference. . . . A career, we can say, demands technical intelligence to learn a skill, to find out how to get from here to there. A calling demands critical intelligence to question whether "there" is worth going toward. . . . [A calling] sees service as the purpose of life . . . . It is not against ambition, but considers ambition a good servant and a bad master.[6]

Staying focused on call is important because so doing brings us back to the spiritual challenge of discerning the ways in which God is calling us and to the ethical dilemma of assigning priority among the several dimensions of call we experience.

Locating One's Call

> *Now there was a great wind, so strong that it was splitting*
> *mountains and breaking rocks in pieces before the LORD, but*
> *the LORD was not in the wind; and after the wind an earth-*
> *quake, but the LORD was not in the earthquake; and after the*
> *earthquake a fire, but the LORD was not in the fire; and after*
> *the fire a sound of sheer silence.*
>
> 1 Kings 19:11b-12

Many factors cause us to be confused about the notion of call. To begin, as a people we are uninterested in the concept. If Alaskan Inuits have four dozen words for snow, our society has at least as many to capture our fascination with self-interest, ambition, and getting ahead. But when pressed to articulate how John Haynes Holmes's stirring hymn "The Voice of God Is Calling" applies to us, or to defend a decision to accept a professional position, even though it will jeopardize our children's educational opportunities, we stammer. Nothing in our society encourages us to penetrate this realm, and most of us, including clergy, avoid it.

The problem is not entirely due to unfamiliarity. When we do examine our callings, we often follow Elijah's path. We look at this or that event and ask ourselves, Was that an indication of God's call? When confronted with a difficult and momentous decision, we ask, Where is the voice of God calling me, in this direction or that one? But the mystery Elijah confronts is that God's presence, God's call, is not where he first expects: in the mighty events that demonstrate nature's power. After the dust settles, the earth steadies, and the fire is quenched, Elijah discovers that God is to be found in the sound of silence.

Practitioners of Discernment

One reason we have such trouble answering the question Whom do you serve? is that the answer propels us, along with Elijah, Abraham (Gen. 22:1-19), Jesus (Matt. 26:39), Dietrich Bonhoeffer, and others, into the realm of paradox.

The way we can increase our confidence that God is calling us to a particular choice is to be persistently, habitually attentive to the voice of God speaking to us in both the sounds and the silences of our lives. If we give constant consideration to whom we serve[7] and redirect our lives again and again toward God, we become practitioners of discernment. We begin to recognize God's signature on some of the choices we embrace, not because the choice corresponds neatly to the answers in the back of some super-saint's book, but because our persistent search for God leads us into a relationship that is confirmed in both subtle and obvious ways.

Thus, the question of discerning a call has to do less with the criteria we cite when we face a huge fork in the road (Is it consistent with scripture? Does it enhance covenants already made?) and more with recognizing God's hand in our decisions at numerous, small forks in the road. To put it another way, discernment is less about clarifying the qualities that authenticate God's activity and more about recognizing, from our point of view, that the call could appear self-contradictory or even physically impossible.[8] The paradox lies in the gulf that exists between God's intentions and our capacity to understand them. We have no bridge that can perfectly cross that gulf.

Lightning East to West

For as the lightning comes from the east and flashes as far as the west, so will be the coming of the Son of Man.
Matthew 24:27

The Gospel of Matthew portrays Jesus in the final days of his life as trying to convey to his disciples an understanding of the intricate way God's presence is woven into all reality—even those events so difficult to face. In this portrayal, is Jesus preparing the disciples for his crucifixion or for the end times? Or, are both dimensions present? In any case, he wants them to be certain that God is present through it all and that, come what may, they should not lose hope but keep looking for the signs of the times. Those signs are as plain as day. They are as obvious as lightning flashing from east to west.

We can recognize when God is calling us only if we orient our lives so that our relationship with God is the context within which we live out all other commitments. Because the issues associated with calling overlap so many other critical issues of our lives, it is difficult to sort out priorities.

We can be truly attentive only when we reconcile ourselves to the fact that everything appealing in life must be understood in the context of God's call.

By grounding ourselves in this way, we prepare ourselves to discern an authentic call from God to initiate a search. That initiative may conflict with other commitments—to our present congregations, to our families, to ongoing projects in our communities, for example. It may reconcile these commitments in a more integrated life. It may even lead to the discovery that we are not called to initiate a search. We must remember that taking the first step of a journey with no particular destination does not bind us to the entire journey, or even to a second step, for that matter. One step at a time. That's good advice throughout the process!

For Your Reflection

- What was your understanding of your call when you decided to accept your current position? How has that understanding changed since you arrived? If possible, map this out in detail, indicating why you believe each of these changes occurred.
- If you are reading this book because you are dissatisfied with your current position, make a list of what you are dissatisfied about—a list of gripes, if you will. Once you have made the list, evaluate each of the complaints, asking of each whether it is an expression of career disappointment or vocational confusion.
- What disciplines of discernment are part of your routine? What do you do to recognize God's active presence and influence in your day-to-day life?
- Review *Discerning God's Will Together*, by Danny Morris and Charles Olsen. If you don't have time to read the whole book, consider the section entitled "Basic Assumptions about Spiritual Discernment."[9]

CHAPTER 2

Overcoming Inertia: What Would Jesus Do?

When it comes to the possibility of looking for a new position, most ministers experience a good deal of inertia. By gaining an understanding of why we are inclined to stay put, we expand our freedom, and we connect more fully to God's active involvement in our current situations and in our futures.

I once sought out a close clergy friend because I was ambivalent about whether or not to update my profile in preparation for a job search. He is a good listener and he heard me out. When I finished, I was hoping he would provide me with some inspiring words or convince me that it was not as difficult as I had made it out to be. Instead, he recalled his own situation a few years earlier. He was in a job he liked, but he knew that he needed to update his profile. He sent away for the papers. When they arrived, he put them on top of his desk so that he would see them every day. There they sat, and sat, and sat, for three years, untouched. Finally he became so angry and disgusted with himself that he put them in his desk drawer. Six months later, he pulled them out and completed his profile.

My friend is not alone. Many times I have been forewarned to expect a profile reference from a colleague who is beginning to put together his or her profile, only to remember months later that it never came. When I have inquired about the process, I have heard one explanation or another of why the person became bogged down.

This kind of inertia, when evident in the life of a clergy, can be overcome only when the proper diagnosis is understood. The problem is spiritual in nature. To grasp this, consider how easy it can be to undertake a task when we believe God is calling us to do it. When our efforts are propelled by divine affirmation, taking the initiative is frequently a joy. Even difficult challenges can be met with confidence.

In contrast, when we are unable to tell whether or not God is calling us to perform a particular task—a task for which we would need God's blessing and support—we can become paralyzed. Beyond the inertia that accompanies ordinary tasks when we are ambivalent, the inertia that accompanies spiritual challenge is even more profound. In two key books that address this area, the need to assess, or reassess, our giftedness is emphasized.[1] In other words, "know thyself" and you will have the energy needed to propel you forward and initiate a search.

While an accurate and rich assessment of our giftedness is crucial to a successful job search, knowledge of our call should not be reduced to clarity about our gifts. Because call comes from outside of ourselves, discernment of call cannot boil down to taking an inventory of our gifts. Rather, beyond such an inventory, we would do well to pray over the following questions:

- Where does God move my heart to use these gifts? And with what circumstances, problems, and groups of people?[2]
- What is God's trajectory for my life? What might God have in mind that I have not dared to dream or imagine? ("Not my will but yours be done" Luke 22:42.)
- When, in the past few years, have I experienced God calling me to undertake something that, were it not for divine affirmation and nudging, I would have avoided? The key here is to get in touch with what it felt like before undertaking the project. On what projects did God's urging prove decisive in motivating me to begin?

These questions ascribe to God agency, a perspective with ethical, theological, and spiritual implications. By orienting our lives in a way that takes into account God's activity in our lives, we approach many of the search process questions differently, particularly the aspect of call.

Why Change?

After identifying God's call as a motivator, the next question we must face is, Why change the status quo? In order to initiate a search, we must embrace change. The impetus for change originates when the three sources of change converge. First, change can be self-generated. Second, change can be prompted by a shift in circumstances that is beyond our control. Third, change can be called out of us through a process or event that transcends both self and surroundings. God can be present in each of these ways, although God's presence in the third is unique.

The first, self-generated change, is prompted by a shift in self-evaluation or a dawning consciousness of a new value we have embraced. This can reveal itself in a variety of ways, including boredom, ambition, or a desire for new challenge.

As clergy, we do not often allow ourselves to look honestly at our own desire to simply move on. Many of us assume that what brought us to our current congregations involved something higher than mere personal choice, or that of the search committee. While this assumption may be so, it is not always the case. And, even if our coming to our current positions was a testimony to God's will, we must take into account that God's will evolves, just as ours does. We do not worship a God who uncritically endorses the status quo. God's endorsement of our current circumstances does not preclude support for change. Thus, it is essential that we take seriously our inner murmurings. They can be reason enough to initiate a search.

The second source of change, a change in circumstances, does not mean that any change, or even any significant change, in circumstances is a good reason to change. In fact, wise counsel suggests that there are many times when our circumstances change and we should not even consider looking for a new position.[3] Nevertheless, a change in circumstances can give rise to a change in call.

I think of a newly installed minister whose infant son died a year or so after he and his family moved to a new church. Although the minister stayed on for a few years, he finally left for a much happier situation. Years later, many said that the death of his child cast such a pall on his family's experience in their new setting that the only thing to do was leave.

The role of minister is demanding in a variety of personal and professional ways. Because of this, our stability (in all senses of the word) greatly depends on the balance we achieve between our personal, home, and professional lives. That balance can be easily upset by a change in our own lives, or the life of someone close to us. For example, a young, single pastor may welcome the opportunity to live in the parsonage that accompanies her new position, but if she marries and has children, she will not likely have the freedom to review nearby school systems when her children enter school. Her congregation will likely expect her to stay in the parsonage, and financial constraints may obligate her to do so. Nevertheless, she must confront the change in her circumstances.

In addition to changes in personal circumstances, things also change in our congregations. Sometimes these are rather obvious changes that would occasion anyone to consider a shift: the departure of a key colleague, a natural disaster that requires an immediate capital campaign of five times the annual budget, a decision by the missions committee to redirect the support of the church from work we find meaningful to work we consider superficial. Even seemingly minor changes can give rise to thoughts about leaving: the congregation's decision to purchase a new hymnal, a key committee chair who is a close personal friend moving away, an ongoing conflict with a colleague or parishioner. Thus, although we may have little or no control over changes in our circumstances, it is important for us to monitor them. Like it or not, they could make it necessary to initiate a search.

In addition to urgings rooted in the self and those rooted in circumstance, our desire for change can originate in an experience of God calling us to change. In my many discussions with colleagues, this is the least common impetus for change. More frequently, ministers report that God works through self-understanding and changing circumstances. But occasionally, God intervenes directly.

In its most dramatic form, this occurs when a minister's life and circumstances are stable, and he or she is otherwise content. Contentment in ministry comes "from standing constantly and consciously in the presence of God so that [God] can transform any task into something meaningful."[4] Just when everything is OK, and we are calmly recognizing God's presence in much of what we do, God may turn our attention from maintaining the status quo to an opportunity to do God's will more fully.

When we are confronted with this type of call, we realize just how compelling God can be.[5] God summons, yet God remains inscrutable. When God calls in this fashion, we answer. "You did not choose me, but I chose you" (John 15:16), Jesus tells his disciples. Paul is blinded on the road to Damascus, and exclaims, "Woe is me if I do not proclaim the gospel" (1 Cor. 9:16). Inertia is no longer an option. The hound of heaven urges us on.

Why Is Change So Difficult?

Even when we know there is good reason to initiate a change, we are often imprisoned by inertia. However individuated the minister may be, there is always a good deal of interdependence with the congregation as meaningful relationships are built. By entertaining even the thought of change, the minister breaks what mutuality has existed and must cope in isolation with feelings of disloyalty. So strong are these feelings that I have heard ministers describe their thoughts about pursuing another call as "dirty."

Ministers can also interpret their desire to seek another call as an expression of excessive ambition. Because few have struggled to understand the complex arena of ambition,[6] many ministers fear any experience that even resembles ambition. When an interest to look at another church emerges, many simply squelch the desire.

Although higher pay and increased benefits motivate lay people to change positions, the world of parish ministry is rather flat when it comes to these quantitative motivations to change. The opportunity is simply not there—or is so only rarely. A top-paid senior minister receives only twice the going rate for a seminarian just out of seminary. In the corporate world, such a ratio is typically 12 to 1, and often much higher. As a result, the costs associated with a move frequently outweigh any possible material benefits. While it is almost inconceivable that a minister would be "in it for the money," most of us do consider the financial picture when we consider a change. And, for most of us, limited prospects for significant material improvement elevate the importance of a wide variety of other considerations.

Finally, fear of the unknown can often produce inertia when considering a change. Even when our current situations are riddled with problems and frustrations, at least these problems are familiar to us. We lived with them as they emerged and developed. In fact, we often contributed to the very problems we seek to leave behind.

In a chapter of *The Active Life*, Parker Palmer notes, "I have sometimes feared life itself, and the movement toward new life, more than I have feared death in its various forms."[7] He makes this point with two stories. The first is a well-known, albeit slightly embellished, dialogue from Woody Allen's *Annie Hall*.

A man goes to a psychiatrist, complaining that his brother-in-law, who lives with him, thinks he is a chicken.

"Describe his symptoms," the doctor says. "Maybe I can help."

"Well," the man replies, "he cackles a lot, he pecks at the rug and the furniture, and he makes nests in the corners."

The doctor thinks for a moment, then says, "It sounds like a simple neurosis to me. Bring your brother-in-law in and I think I can cure him completely."

"Oh no, Doc. We wouldn't want that. We need the eggs!"[8]

The other story, more somber, is an apocryphal tale about the apostle Peter.

Immediately after the crucifixion and resurrection of Jesus, Peter, filled with the power of this great event, sees a blind beggar crouched in the dust beside the city gate. Overcome with compassion, Peter rushes to the man, places his hands over the blind man's eyes, and says, "In the name of the resurrected Christ, may your sight be restored!"

The beggar leaps to his feet, eyes wide open and clearly healed. But with his face full of rage he screams at Peter, "You fool! You have destroyed my way of making a living!" In one swift and violent motion, the beggar gouges out his eyes with his own thumbs and collapses into the street.[9]

Anxiety about new challenges, new responsibilities, and new circumstances in which we must prove ourselves can be powerful. Yet what kind of understanding of God is compatible with such fears? It is difficult to imagine that a person held captive by fear could view God as an active agent in the world, or for that matter, that he or she could integrate Jesus' persistent refrain that love casts out all fear. All the more reason for ministers to practice regularly spiritual disciplines that remind them of their gifts[10] and of the many ways God might desire to use them.

For Your Reflection

- Think about the last time you experienced God calling you to undertake a new task or turn your life in a certain direction. Was it difficult or easy to initiate? What about the experience gave you confidence that it was God who was calling you to do this?
- Do you believe God was involved in bringing you to your current call? How did you experience God's involvement?
- What have been the most disturbing changes at your church since you have arrived? Make a list. Are any of these changes so significant that they constitute a legitimate reason to consider initiating a search?

- If you have been considering initiating a search for a long time, what has been holding you back? Look over the last few pages of this chapter and highlight what sounds familiar. Where has God been as you have been waiting to initiate your search?

CHAPTER 3

Responses to Getting the Itch

At some point in time, most of us will experience an intrusion into our state of being. Into our already full and complicated lives will come the realization that there might be something better out there. How we respond to this thought affects both our discipleship and our contentment.

Once the thought of leaving our current churches has entered our minds, the relationship with our current congregations is never the same. This is not to say we are destined to leave in the hope of finding greener pastures. After all, we may discover new ways to engage ministry in our current settings. But many who entertain the possibility of change find it is no longer possible to commit totally to the tasks at hand. Instead, depending on our threshold, at some point we begin to ask if it is all worth it. We wonder if another church would appreciate our gifts more thoroughly. We increasingly dwell on conflicts or impediments. We find it difficult to ignore criticisms or accusations we would have brushed off a year ago.

While imperfect in many ways, the metaphor of marriage is one way to describe the relationship between a minister and his or her congregation.[1] Once a married man or woman seriously considers leaving a spouse, the relationship is never the same. It may mature by dealing directly with the circumstances that gave rise to this possibility, it may slip into soulless mediocrity,[2] or it may dissolve either amicably or rancorously.

In this way, from the moment we open ourselves to the possibility of an alternative call, we serve two masters: the continuing sense that we are called to advance God's purposes in our current congregations and the emerging sense that we must attend to the new opportunity God may be calling us to explore. This dilemma is best resolved when a variety of alternatives are considered.

Staying Put

Pastoral ministry is such a multidimensional and challenging vocation that it should not be surprising when a minister is haunted by thoughts of moving on. The scrutiny, the expectations, the relentless deadlines, the meaning we hold for our parishioners—all of these realities remain true even if we initiate a search.

When we get the itch to move on, for whatever reason, it is critical that we stop and take a long, prayerful look. Why? Why now? Chapter 1 outlined many of the circumstances that might occasion these thoughts. Once we understand the origins of change, we must look at all the alternatives available to us.

Most of these alternatives involve staying put. What follows is a partial list of responses, any of which might be an alternative for a particular minister. Not all of these options will be available or accessible to all ministers. Nevertheless, each of us must realize that even though leaving our current church might be our *first* thought, it should not be our only thought. In fact, it may not be our best thought.

Take a Sabbatical

In an era of tightening budgets and diminishing benefits, it seems more and more difficult to include sabbatical time in a minister's contract. Yet, as we become increasingly overwhelmed with business and the pace of modern life, a sabbatical becomes increasingly important.

When we get the itch to leave our present settings, a sabbatical can offer perspective. Taking an inventory of one's life and situation takes time. We may want to speak with friends, read books that encourage us to reflect on our circumstances, attend a workshop to help us sort through our thoughts and feelings, or take a retreat to reconnect with the Holy One. For all of these purposes, the time a sabbatical offers and the resulting perspective gained can be critical.

Begin a Doctor of Ministry Degree

While our jobs as parish ministers require us to be fairly well read and to have a thorough knowledge of scripture and theology, we are not specialists.

Many of us are malnourished from a steady diet of countless, routine tasks and endless situations where our counsel is needed. Although our perspectives and wisdom are valued, we rarely have a chance to pursue anything in much depth.

A doctorate of ministry (D.Min.) can change that. What may at first sound like a call to look to another congregation might in fact be an eagerness to explore a particular project at a depth our usual pastoral ministries do not require and cannot abide.

Congregations are generally supportive of ministers who initiate a D.Min. program. Parishioners want to be confident that their minister is well educated, always learning and growing, and up-to-date. This is not to say that negotiating the time to focus on studying and writing will come easily. Nevertheless, initiating a D.Min. program is usually received positively.

A good D.Min. experience can have a variety of effects. On the one hand, it may reassure us that our current congregations are just where we should stay. On the other hand, it may deepen our longing and thus diminish our commitment to our current congregations, relegating our normal ministerial duties to the back seat.

Identify Your Passion: Launch a New Ministry in Your Church

Richard Nelson Bolles, an expert at job searches, reminds us of an oft-quoted observation by Frederick Buechner: "The place God calls you to is the place where your deep gladness and the world's deep hunger meet."[3] For many, the itch to look elsewhere is marked either by the loss of this sense of "deep gladness" from their present ministries or by a lack of involvement in a ministry or mission that addresses the "deep hunger" of the world.

Most ministers know what Buechner is referring to. Most of us have been blessed with one or more times in our lives when we have been overwhelmed with gratitude while addressing the significant needs of others. So, when we lack this sense of gladness and satisfaction in our current settings, looking for a different position is not always the obvious first step. What may feel like a desire to leave our current settings may really be a desire to engage our current calls in a new way.

This sounds easier than it is. Because the job of being a minister is never finished, few of us have spare time on our hands. If we launch a new ministry in our current churches, we will have to do other things differently. This will create stress, and it will likely attract criticism. Nevertheless, no price is too great to pay if a minister who is lost rediscovers his or her call.[4]

A new ministry or mission can also prompt the congregation to examine its overall mission and ministry. Leading this process can help clarify our own calls, role as minister, and relationships to our current congregations.

Consider the Span of Your Call

I have spoken with many clergy who are in the midst of long-term pastorates. Most of them have been tempted on numerous occasions to consider going to another church. What these ministers have in common is that in exploring the possibility of leaving, they learned that they are called to live out their ministries in one place, not unlike the vow taken by Benedictine monks. While some fall into a lifelong position by way of inertia, many choose this path as an expression of their understanding of God's call.

One of the distinctive features of parish ministry is that if we choose to claim them, we have multiple opportunities to show initiative. Staying in one place is a possibility because ministering to a particular congregation can be ever changing, ever deepening, ever rewarding. I know ministers who have served as public officials (including school board members) and in the U.S. House of Representatives (for example, Rev. Walter Faunteroy, former representative from the District of Columbia), chaired local non-profits' boards of directors, and written editorials for local newspapers. Such ministries are not usually available to a pastor who stays only five years in each congregation.

Of course, a long-term pastorate is not for everyone. If it is to be fruitful and rewarding, ministers must be confident that their staying expresses both God's will and their own. This confidence cannot be achieved by repressing the urge to look elsewhere. It can only be won by fully entering into the consideration of other calls, only to discover what T. S. Eliot said so eloquently:

> We shall not cease from exploration
> And the end of all our exploring
> Will be to arrive where we started
> And know the place for the first time.[5]

Going Fishing

In addition to choosing to "stay put," we might also decide to "go fishing," a response that makes manifest the problems associated with "serving two masters."

Even the decision to update our profiles is complicated because it forces us to deal with the spiritual challenge of being true to our individual calls, even though it seems that doing so will distract us from serving our current congregations. Additionally, it necessitates that we deal with the awkwardness and potential ethical compromises entailed in assembling our profiles. Specifically, asking members of our current congregations to complete references for us will likely raise in their minds and hearts questions we may be unable to answer (because we are not yet clear about what caused our initiation) or unwilling to answer fully (because we think that revealing our desire to pursue another position would be ill-advised).

Loren Mead echoes the advice of many when he reminds pastors who have just decided to seek another position to "Do your [current] job."[6] This requires emphasis because it is so difficult, both practically and spiritually, to seek another call while fulfilling one's current call.

Frequently ministers become disinterested or disenchanted with their present positions once they have begun a search. On a purely practical basis, initiating a search can have disastrous consequences for one's present ministry, one's potential for landing a meaningful call, and one's spirit. As ministers, we are often spiritually ill-equipped to maintain a high level of commitment in our current situations once we sense that we are called to look seriously at other choices. How can we continue to minister effectively in such a situation?

Paradise Lost

There was a time in our current settings when we actually looked forward to committee meetings, when we welcomed the opportunity to write the weekly newsletter column so that we could make an important point, when preparing a sermon for the eighteenth Sunday after Pentecost in Year A was a welcomed challenge, and when we were honored and genuinely excited when an associate wanted our advice. Perhaps it's a stretch to refer to this as "paradise." But most of us find a good bit of fulfillment in the everyday experiences of ministry.

Once a minister embarks on revising his or her profile, however, a new kind of energy emerges. But all too often, the excitement is gone from our current settings. Wm. Bud Phillips offers a penetrating analysis of the variety of ways in which ministers end their relationships with congregations. Building on the work of William Bridges,[7] Phillips calls them disenchantment, dis-identification, disorganization, and disengagement. His use of illustrations makes it easy to apply his insight to one's own situation.[8]

What he does not do is offer help in ministering authentically in one's current situation while actively pursuing the possibility of another call. As we write our sermons; sit in endless committee meetings; supervise staff; tinker with the computers and the sound system; negotiate with the nursery director; adjust the thermostat, boiler, or air conditioners; and occasionally shovel the walks; how will we as dedicated servants of God continue to devote ourselves to our current churches when our minds and hearts are simultaneously being pulled in another direction?

Understanding Call from God's Perspective

Few, if any, ministers perceive an unambiguous call from God, follow it, and are never tempted to look elsewhere. Even so, many ministers are quite fulfilled spending their entire lives ministering in one setting. On the surface, it looks like God's call to them was straightforward and relatively uncomplicated: "Go there. Stay there. Use all your gifts to minister there." But life this side of heaven is more complex than that.

Those who remain fulfilled in a single call work with God to discover ways they might expand their ministries, evolve in their self-understanding, and integrate new directions and activities into their present settings. Their calls evolve, too. What distinguishes these ministers is that they find a way, in dialog with God, to embrace their evolving calls while remaining in a single setting.

Far more common are we clergy who experience God's call to consider ministering in a new setting. Although exploring that call may catapult us into conflict and tension, the call itself begins yet another manifestation of God's multidimensional grace.

A crucial lesson of both the New and Old Testaments is that God does not operate within our tidy or comfortable definitions. God is free. Out of freedom emerges what to us first appears as chaos, contradiction, and paradox. The challenge is not to stop there. Discernment involves the ultimate trust that, although we can never know the mind of God, the intention to give ourselves over to God's will can result in gaining a life direction that expresses God's will.

What we do know is that God does not operate like a film editor, always making a clean cut from one scene to another. What we don't know is how to live in both scenes at once. I would suggest that the only answer is to receive God's nurturing grace, which is present even in the midst of our confusion and conflict. As we do so, we expand our capacity to understand our lives from God's perspective. And in the end, is that not the answer to all our questions?

For Your Reflection

- Before initiating a search, take the time to thoroughly consider alternatives that involve staying put.
  - Have you considered asking for a sabbatical? What is holding you back?
  - Identify the area of ministry you would most enjoy over the next several years. Then look for D.Min. programs that would encourage such a focus.
  - Gain perspective on your current position and ask yourself, What new ministry could I launch at my current church that would energize me and address needs that are presently underserved?
  - Seek out a colleague who has been at his or her current call for more than fifteen years and plans to retire there. Ask him or her about the benefits of a long-term pastorate and about strategies to avoid growing stale.

- Set aside some time each day—especially when you find yourself unmotivated in your current job—to pray on Jesus' words in the garden: "Yet, not my will but yours be done" (Luke 22:42).
- If you are feeling bored or disinterested in your current congregation, try this: Contemplate what it means to be a servant as you reflect on your duties in your current job. Remind yourself of the trust, the hope, and the dreams that your current congregation has invested in your leadership. While you squarely face your feelings of boredom or

disinterest, open yourself to the ways God continues to call you in your current congregation. If you are itching to look for a new position because your current call no longer holds the power that was once so compelling, not only is it essential that you assemble your profile, but also that you open yourself to a new understanding of your current position.

CHAPTER 4

Leaving Our Current Congregations in the Dark

The more complex the actual situations of a man's life, the more responsible and the more difficult will be his task of "telling the truth."

Dietrich Bonhoeffer, *Ethics*

The decision to pursue a position at another church will almost inevitably thrust us onto the horns of a dilemma. The effectiveness of ministry depends entirely on the presence of trust and authenticity. And if we undermine that trust, we will almost certainly scuttle our ministry. However, with rare exception,[1] we will find it necessary to deceive members of our current congregations about our intentions and actions. This occurs in spite of our ordination vow to "be zealous in maintaining both the truth of the gospel and the peace of the church, speaking the truth in love."[2]

Literature on the ministerial search process offers no help. In fact, nothing published to date even addresses the topic of deception, an issue almost every minister and congregation will face many times. Is it possible to engage a search process and avoid deceiving our current congregation?

Can Deceit Be Avoided?

In all of my discussions and reading, I have encountered only one case where a minister simply announced to his congregation that the time had come for him to begin a search for a new situation. He told them his reasons. He told them that most searches take between one and three years.

And he promised he would continue to minister to them faithfully throughout the process. In questioning him, I was unable to identify any characteristics peculiar to his circumstance that made this unusual situation possible. Instead, I became even more aware that each of us serves in a unique situation and has a unique relationship with our congregations. What may be possible in one place is not possible in many other situations.

What keeps us from following the path of openness? Are there reasons why this path is not so well worn? A sampling of reasons follows:

- "I would become a lame duck." A strong mutual sense of commitment between minister and congregation is necessary for an effective ministry. Once the minister tells the congregation that he or she is intending to leave, the congregation is left without a full partner. And congregants will make their disappointment known.
- "The 'love affair' would be over." The relationship between a congregation and its minister is governed by mutual love, admiration, and respect. If congregants leave or stop attending in large numbers, it communicates a problem to the minister. Likewise, if the minister voices his or her intention to leave, it communicates a problem to the congregation.
- "In the face of conflict, I would lose any leverage I have with staff and lay leaders." Not only is such leverage a result of interaction consistently rooted in the truth, it results when all parties recognize that they must work together indefinitely. If the minister declares an intention to leave, the future is no longer indefinite. The "other side" can simply wait out the conflict until the minister leaves.
- "My family would be unnecessarily subjected to all the ups and downs of a search with no role in effecting an outcome." Anything said openly to the entire congregation will soon be known to the minister's family, including young children. Few congregants hesitate to discuss a minister's personal life, even in front of his or her family. Thus, it is often wise to keep the details of a search private. Certainly it would be inappropriate to saddle a young child with the anxiety of a potential move when, in fact, the process could take years and could result in no move at all.

For these reasons, and many more, the vast majority of us do not tell our current congregations that we are initiating a search. Thus, we must contend with the complexities created by one or another level of deception.

Deception: Ethical Considerations

> *It is obviously a most effective protection for legitimate se-*
> *crets that it should be universally understood and expected*
> *that those who ask questions which they have no right to ask*
> *will have lies told to them.*
> H. Sidgwick, *The Methods of Ethics*

What questions do congregants have "no right to ask" and who decides what these are? Who communicates to congregations—and how—what these questions are and that they are "off-limits"? Numerous authors and organizations (including the Alban Institute) are developing seminars and books that focus on norms for Christian behavior in congregations in hopes of building an understanding of the pastor's need for privacy in his or her search for a new position. Nevertheless, it is crucial that we closely monitor our actions and our motives as we enter this process. What follows is a review and evaluation of some of the more common ways we justify acts of deception, which we would condemn under virtually any other circumstance.

It's Only a White Lie

Some ministers will defend secretive activity by describing it as nothing more than a "white lie." The problem with all white lies, of course, is that "they spread so easily, and that lines are very hard to draw."[3] A congregation is extremely vulnerable to its minister's abuse of trust. Newspapers and tabloids in the past two decades provide ample evidence of those once-mighty clergy who have fallen. Choosing to regard what we say in this circumstance as a "white lie" trivializes the importance of the minister-congregation relationship, thereby creating the possibility of more "white lies" in the future.

It's My Life, Thank You Very Much!

Life in a congregation is a lot like life in a small town, especially for the minister and his or her family. Because privacy is so scarce, veteran ministers often zealously guard what little privacy they have. There is enormous variation on this issue. Whether or not a minister can be open depends upon the relationship he or she has with the congregation. A congregation may have a free and flowing relationship with one minister yet find her successor defensive and excessively private. Likewise, a minister may be relatively open with one congregation yet keep to himself with another.

Regardless of whether we ministers guard our privacy in everyday life, many of us will choose to keep our decision to initiate a search private. Like public officials, we have private lives and we have an obligation to our loved ones (and perhaps to ourselves) to maintain that privacy. In an in-depth examination of these issues well worth reading, Brandeis University professor Sissela Bok points out that our right to withhold information about our personal plans and motives is not the same as a right to lie about them.[4] Morally, that leaves us with the favorite option of many public figures, "no comment," which is clearly out of the question for a minister. Imagine saying to a parishioner who asks if you are circulating your profile, "I'd rather not talk about that." When our flock is also our boss, we cannot afford such a distant and aloof response.

Ask a Stupid Question, Expect a Stupid Answer

Recalling Sidgwick's comment at the beginning of this section, a legitimate secret is protected by the fact that those who are "too nosey" will have lies told to them. Of course, Sidgwick's assumption is that this principle is universally understood, for our purposes among the congregation. The problem is, the most "nosey" members of a congregation are the least likely to recognize that they have no right to a truthful response.

Sorry, But I Can't Say Anything Just Now

Another rationale is to withhold comment on the grounds that letting our congregations know about our initiation of a search would be harmful—to us, to the present and immediate future of our current congregations, and to our search process. Eventually we will tell them, of course.[5] But to tell them now would serve no purpose and, for many of our parishioners, might call into question the integrity of our relationships with them.

We may succeed at being evasive ("Well, the thought has crossed my mind."), but most likely we will have to lie, at least until the dust settles. And it's worth considering just how long that might be. If the average search takes about two years, and the average length of a parish minister's stay is about five years, it is important to realize that as much as 40 percent of our time as parish ministers might be spent under these morally awkward circumstances.

The effects of deceit—whether evasion, secrecy, or telling white lies— are subtle. Congregants will sense it long before they explicitly speak of it, and they will speak to one another long before they speak with us. What's more, a vague sense that "something is going on" could cause a governing board to back away from an exciting initiative or cause a potential leader of the church to decline nomination.

Even after we have departed for our next congregations, the effects of deceit can be felt. Indeed, many congregants will remember that we lied about whether or not we were engaged in a search without ever understanding why we felt compelled to do so. Not only is that a legacy no minister would want, but it also detracts in advance from the trust our successors will seek to establish in their first few years of ministry.

The Risks of Secrecy

It is important here to reflect on some of the ways privacy can be compromised and trust breached in a search. No matter how carefully we try to control how, when, and by whom details of our situation will be publicized, ultimately we must depend upon the good judgment of both close associates and the colleagues we encounter in the search process. The following is an unusual situation, but it reveals some of the myriad ways secrecy could backfire.

Imagine a minister, five months after arriving at her new congregation, realizing that she has made a terrible decision and must find a new call. Luckily, she updated her profile just before she received this call, so it was less than a year old. After identifying ten potential congregations, she writes a personal letter to the head of each search committee, explaining her circumstances, informing them that her profile (which does not include mention of her present position) will be sent to them, and asking that they speak with no one in her present congregation since they would be upset to learn that she is considering leaving after only a few months. She speaks with her former congregation references listed on her profile to let them know what she is doing and asks them not to speak with anyone in her present congregation. The committee accepts her explanation, satisfied to speak only to the references on her profile, and she secures an interview. The committee abides by her request not to visit her present setting and invites her to a neutral pulpit. She impresses them favorably, and they extend a call to her.

In the real world, search committees, while sometimes gullible, are usually suspicious of any candidate who departs from the norm. The initial phase of their work focuses on discarding applicants. This minister's letter would raise eyebrows: "What is the real story? Do we even want to consider pursuing someone in this situation?" The brevity of her stay at her current congregation would raise serious questions as to her loyalty. In fact, the committee's suspicion might cause it to breach confidentiality by asking her references why she is leaving her current position. Committee members might phone people in her present community, or even the president or moderator of her current congregation. In short, the security of this or any secret can come undone in countless ways.

A Better Approach

Interim ministers sometimes focus their first sermon on saying good-bye. This makes it clear from the start that their time with the congregation will be limited, and that whatever they hope to accomplish must be done in a relatively brief period of time. If a permanently called minister were to do this, it would focus undue attention on the end of the relationship, at a time when hopes for the future are still developing.[6]

All clergy will be asked with some frequency, directly and indirectly, how long we think we will stay. Our responses to such questions are crucial because they represent a natural opportunity, free from the pressure of an impending search, to provide congregants with a gentle reminder of what they already know: that no relationship this side of heaven will last forever. If we plant the seeds of our eventual departure early on, our relationships with our congregations will be more real and therefore more healthy.

By addressing the issue throughout our ministries, however obliquely, do we thereby avoid deception when we enter an active search? In fact, being open about our intention to leave eventually alters the context. Rather than an indication of disloyalty or abandonment, our decision to leave becomes a matter of timing. If we do this well and consistently, without raising questions of loyalty and commitment, when the time comes we will honestly be able to say that we are not deceiving the congregation by initiating a search "behind their backs." Rather, we are doing exactly what we told them we would.

Seeking References from Our Current Congregations

One of the reasons we have such trouble updating our profiles is that it is difficult to know what to say when the congregants we ask to be our references question if we're leaving and why. Whatever we say to them will make our relationships with them different from our relationships with other members of the congregation. Depending on our approach, that is, whether we choose a furtive or open path in initiating a search, we may say that we are entrusting them with a secret or we may characterize our preparation of a profile as a routine task that all ministers (at least ought to) perform. Regardless of our strategy, however, from that day forward, the congregants we approach will likely suspect that "something is going on" and wonder what lies ahead.

Put simply, beginning a search is never an easy, straightforward matter, because our relationships with congregants are rooted in fidelity and trust. The very act of preparing a profile threatens that fidelity. Doing it secretively threatens that trust.

Nevertheless, we are rightly expected to supply any potential search committee with up-to-date references. This requires us to approach a select group of congregants and ask them to enter into a different type of relationship with us. Such conversations can be conducted in different ways, of course, depending on personal style and comfort level. Whatever the style used, the following guidelines will always be of benefit:

- Rehearse each conversation several times before you contact the congregant. Focus in particular on what you do *not* feel comfortable telling him or her and rehearse answers that will enable you to avoid divulging those things.
- Decide what your basic explanation will be. Keep it consistent among all congregants with whom you speak. Anticipate questions your explanation may arouse and rehearse your responses. For example, be prepared to answer the question, "Why are you doing this now?"

- Focus specifically on the possibility that you will be asked questions about timing. Be clear about reference deadlines and ask if that date is reasonable.
- Explain to each congregant reference why you have chosen him or her.[7]
- If you'd like the congregant to emphasize a particular talent or strength in the reference, be specific and straightforward in "coaching" him or her.
- Discuss how the congregant should respond if someone else in the congregation confronts him or her with the rumor that you are seeking another position. This may be the most difficult part of the conversation, so it is best for you to take the initiative.
- Follow-up is critical. Maintain clear records about whom you contacted and when, how each person responded, which materials you provided, and when you received each reference. Write each congregant a thank-you note and reiterate anything from your discussion that might be important to reinforce.

Only after we have been immersed in these preparations for some time can we begin to take to heart the impact these conversations will have on the congregants we contact and on our own frame of mind. No matter how much thinking about "moving on" we may have done up to this point, the first time we ask a parishioner to write a reference is sobering.

If this moment brings us to the realization that we are entering holy ground, then our preparations are complete. The most we can hope for in these conversations is that something of the sacred quality that has governed our behavior and guided our relationship with our congregation since we arrived will continue—however changed—after the veil has been lifted and everyone realizes that their minister will be leaving.

For ourselves, we can hope that God's love, which has inspired and motivated us to devote ourselves to our current congregations, will continue to be tangible to us amidst this transition. During the many months our profiles are circulating, we will grow more accustomed to coping as we seek to serve two masters. But for now, it is challenging. Wisdom suggests that we seek help. In addition to prayer, we will want to consult some trusted confidants. That is the subject of the next chapter.

For Your Reflection

- When was the last time you were asked, "How long are you planning on staying at your current position?" What was your response? If you had to do it over again (and you will!), would you answer differently?
- Think back to conversations you have had with parishioners about confidential or sensitive issues—topics that have nothing to do with your search. Did you choose to be evasive when you were put on the spot? Why? Were other choices available to you at the time? Did you perceive them as real choices? What were the consequences of your evasion, so far as you know?
- After pondering some of the risks involved in initiating a search and reflecting on how the equilibrium we may enjoy in our current congregations can quickly tilt off balance, do you think the trade-off is worth it? Is the motivation for your search sufficiently authentic to justify the risk?

CHAPTER 5

Consultation:
To Whom Can the Minister Turn?

"One of the cardinal sins of clergy seems to be the lone-ranger syndrome in which men and women in ministry keep their most powerful thoughts and feelings to themselves, especially their pain and confusion."[1]

Ministers do not seek out the perspective and help of others often enough. Whatever the reason for this, there are many circumstances in which the counsel of others is enormously beneficial. Other people see things differently than we do, and it is that difference we need most when faced with a dilemma. For example, if we found ourselves presented with a life-threatening psychological crisis, we would not try to go it alone. Or if we had an employee problem that disrupted the life of the church, most of us would seek advice on the appropriate legal action. Yet, when it comes to the challenge of facing a new call, we think we're on our own.

We should realize that our decision to initiate the search process, although part of the regular mix of things in the secular world, is a big deal in the world of parish ministry. The relationships between players are too complex, the possible outcomes for the people and institutions we serve are too unpredictable, and the impact on our life and the lives of our loved ones is too enormous to attempt to manage this entire process on our own—not to mention simultaneously fulfilling our current responsibilities in so sincere and thorough a way as not to raise suspicions among parishioners or colleagues.

Even our circumstances (most of which distinguish us from those in the secular workforce) severely constrain our options. For starters, most of us have spent precious little time cultivating close friendships outside our professional circles and congregations.[2] We work many nights and most weekends, when the rest of the world is available for socializing. Another constraint is our work environment. Only in very large churches are there enough ministerial peers to risk having a confidential discussion about initiating a search without significantly raising anxiety among staff.

In a church with three ordained ministers, one senior minister told his two associates that, from time to time, he considers the possibility of leaving. They were completely taken aback. Days later, they let him know that their sense of job stability and security hinged largely on his continuing leadership. The fact is, the world of ministerial searches is so peculiar that very few people could intelligently advise us on the process.

Last, but certainly not least, as ministers, we are practiced at keeping the confidences of others. Most of us have very little practice at letting others into our confidence.

Despite these constraints, we need community to discern God's will. As Danny Morris and Charles Olsen discuss in their excellent book, *Discerning God's Will Together*, discernment is not the work of an isolated individual. Just as we tell our parishioners when they seek our help in making a difficult decision, we all need the perspective of others whose views and wisdom we value.

The challenge is that the very community we have labored to develop is not available to us as we seek advice or understanding about this particular decision.[3] Obviously it is inappropriate for us to speculate with members of our current congregation about beginning a search that is likely to result in our leaving the congregation. To do so would be to expect the congregant to join us in our consternation, with all its ups and downs. While it is fitting to ask and expect this of a spouse, a congregant is not in a position to be an active participant in the unfolding of circumstances. This imbalance creates a situation in which the minister holds all the cards and the congregant knows only that he or she doesn't want the minister to leave. These circumstances, as well as countless issues surrounding the prospect of our departure, set the stage for, at best, cloudy responses from congregants.

So if the very people with whom we have shared so much of our lives cannot help us on this critical and lonely phase in our journey, who can?[4]

Spiritual Directors, Outside Supervisors, and Pastoral Counselors

A high percentage of the ministers I know have at one time or another sought the services of a therapist or pastoral counselor for personal reasons, including marital and family conflicts, depression, and personal growth. Few are engaged in an ongoing relationship with a spiritual director, outside supervisor, or pastoral counselor to address ongoing professional issues, however. As ministers, we are all supervisors, of volunteers or professional staff or both. We learn in seminary the importance of professional development, but few of us make the time for it in our own weekly schedules. Fewer still have the funds to cover it in our church budgets.

Each of us should have an ongoing relationship with a trusted professional outside our congregations. The purpose of this relationship: to provide us with insightful feedback about our frustrations, personal and professional growth, and so on. Such a relationship will not only keep us accountable, which will reduce our likelihood of falling to temptations such as inappropriate sexual relationships, it will enable us to develop a better understanding of how we can reduce unproductive conflict. Finally, having an established relationship like this can be enormously helpful if and when we consider a new call.

When a voice from within begins to whisper thoughts of looking elsewhere, we are in a precarious position. There is work to be done—spiritual, ethical, and professional—if we are to sort through these thoughts and feelings. That work can best be done with a professional who already knows us well.

These are not trivial matters. Talking with dozens of ministers who have gone through the throes of seeking a new assignment has convinced me that considering a new call can challenge a minister with endless spiritual, theological, psychological, and emotional questions. The dramatic record of one such minister is available in Chandler W. Gilbert's "On Living the Leaving."[5] Gilbert's journal reveals the pain he experienced following his sixtieth birthday and how that pain manifested itself in his physical, spiritual, personal, and professional life. He wrestled to figure out whether his problem was internal or external. He had escapist thoughts and much anxiety. When his dreams temporarily departed, he became forgetful and neglectful. He pondered God's will amidst his pain and finally announced his departure. His journal traces the freedom, anger, and dread that followed.

While Gilbert's circumstances are unique, the feelings and thoughts he articulates are common to many of us who have heard a voice from within calling for change.

As Gilbert found out, we need more than a journal if we are to address the difficult issues and intense pressures of a search. It is foolish to think it won't happen to us. Even if we think we have a solid grasp on the situation and on our relationships with God, having a professional on whom we can rely and in whom we can confide can give us the perspective we need as our lives are unfolding.

Spouse

If we are married or are in a long-term, committed relationship, it is almost certain that we will have the benefit of a spouse's or life partner's counsel at every point along the way.[6] Because our spouses are "interested parties," at many levels, most of us share with them our consternation and decisions, our acceptances and our rejections, our most hopeful and most diabolical thoughts, and the roller coaster of emotions that any search will bring.

We ignore at our peril the fact that our spouses have an independent roller coaster on which they are riding. Sometimes their slow, positive progression up a challenging hill coincides with our own. At other times, they plummet while we rise slowly on a different part of the track. There will be times when we feel we need to spend time together, to discuss options or unburden ourselves of frustration. But it will not always be the case that our spouses will be able to listen right at that moment.

In few other decisions in our adult lives is the range of impact so wide, affecting our own lives and especially the lives of our families. And in few other professions is the decision to change jobs burdened with so much freight, especially if we have a family. A few examples:

- Many churches own a parsonage and expect their minister to live in it. Thus, a decision to take the job is also a decision to live in a specific house. Even if there is no parsonage, it is generally expected that the minister will live in the town where the church is located, regardless of the quality of its school system or employment opportunities for our spouses.

- The position brings with it all sorts of anticipated and unanticipated expectations of a minister's family. For example, family members may be expected to join and participate in the local Scout troop, or other clubs or civic organization. Our spouses may be expected to drive a certain type of car or entertain with some frequency.
- School-age children will be expected to attend public school. If they don't, we will have a lot of explaining to do—and no amount of explaining will justify our decision in the minds of many.

The role of a spouse in the search process is complex and critically important from beginning to end. Because spousal relationships are so unique, and often complicated, there is little universal advice to be offered in this arena. At the end of this chapter, I have included some observations and questions that may bring some important considerations to the surface.

Colleagues and Middle Judicatory Minister

Colleagues can be a most helpful resource. They, more than anyone else, are likely to understand. They know the territory. They've been there. Most are good listeners and are practiced at offering sage advice. They understand confidentiality and are generally among the most trustworthy professionals around. All of this suggests that our colleagues can serve as a rich resource of support and advice, especially if we are able and willing to voice the questions that most trouble us.

Still, there are legitimate reasons for caution. Except in the largest cities, our colleagues interact with many of the same people we do. And, because we are known leaders in our communities, people recognize that we are often privy to information beyond that on the public's horizon, and they often do not hesitate to put us on the spot. In addition, our professional lives are often intertwined with the lives of our local colleagues. We work together on projects and committees. We cover for each other when we go on vacation. We may depend upon each other for friendship and support. Because of this, we may be less than objective in responding to news that our colleague and friend is contemplating a move.

This, too, underscores the importance of maintaining close relationships with colleagues who do not presently live in our communities. Colleagues in distant communities can fulfill our need for friendship and support, and we do not have to apply the same cautions we attach to our local colleagues. And, of course, being able to turn to colleagues who have known us as we have moved through many settings can result in far more perspective and wisdom than most new relationships can offer.[7]

One particular relationship deserves emphasis here. The vast majority of us will turn to our middle judicatory ministers for a reference in the search process. One middle judicatory minister told me that between 90 and 95 percent of the ministers in his area ask him to be a reference. Experienced middle judicatory ministers have seen a lot of searches and, along the way, have become privy to the pitfalls of the process. In his book *Saying Goodbye*, Ed White writes that during his 21 years as a middle judicatory minister, he saw 91 ministers leave their congregations unhappily.[8]

Because middle judicatory ministers must relate to between 50 and 100 congregations, not to mention 100 or more clergy, we cannot expect from them as much as we can from a spiritual director. Furthermore, their commitment in the search process is not restricted to supporting the candidate. Rather, they seek to enhance the possibility of a good match, functioning both as pastor to the pastors and as a placement officer. Middle judicatory ministers often function as teammates, standing by our sides in the midst of struggle. One of their highest priorities is assisting ministers who are in the midst of a search process.

We are well advised if we seek out their wealth of experience, particularly when it comes to potential problems. While they may not volunteer their reflections, most are glad to respond to specific questions. Ministers would do well to draft a list of questions focusing either on their own weaknesses or on the qualities of the particular congregation they are courting. The middle judicatory minister will likely offer helpful insights.

Of course, just as there is great variation among ministers, there is great variation among middle judicatory ministers. It is incumbent upon us to assess the gifts and experience offered by our particular middle judicatory ministers so that we can invite them to join us in a way that takes advantage of their own particular gifts.

Seminars and Workshops

Many workshops focus on concerns that are relevant to an impending search.[9] Because most churches support their minister's desire to attend conferences, it is unlikely that any suspicion will be aroused simply by attending such a conference. Often the greatest benefit comes from the personal connections made with other participants. Their stories can be instructive for our own situations.

In addition to myriad workshops offered by The Alban Institute and various church career development centers,[10] it would be good to develop a workshop for clergy who are just beginning a search. Not only would such a workshop offer clergy guidance of the type this book seeks to articulate, but it would facilitate the sharing of stories and lessons learned by participants so that all could benefit.

For Your Reflection

- Start a list of people, who are not in your parish or living in your current area, to whom you can turn as you go through the search process. It's best to identify positive people who will provide encouragement.
- If you are initiating a search and do not have an ongoing relationship with an outside supervisor, spiritual director, or pastoral counselor, consider establishing such a relationship. The time to begin this relationship is before you begin the search process so that the relationship will have a footing against which the waves of change can pound.
- Draft a list of questions to ask your middle judicatory minister. Seek his or her honest feedback about your weaknesses and your strengths. Ask about your reputation in your diocese or conference. If he or she is familiar with the congregation you are courting, try to gain as much information as you can.

For Those with a Spouse or Significant Other

- Keeping anything about the search from your spouse or life partner is generally a bad idea. Your spouse has a right to know what is going on. He or she is an interested party in your search. In addition, your spouse cares for you and wants to support you. Your spouse knows you (sometimes better than you know yourself) and can offer privileged advice.

- Telling absolutely everything to your spouse is also a bad idea. Any major decision in which one seeks to know God's will is difficult. In particular, the search for a new ministerial position will take you (your thoughts, your emotions, your spirit) to rarely visited places of excitement and despair. It is difficult enough for your spouse to be at least a half-step removed from the one who is the primary actor in this drama. To add to that an expectation that he or she ride every wave to its crest or crash is too much.

- Be as clear as possible with your spouse that your discussions about the search are confidential. Usually a minister's spouse has a good understanding of what is and what is not confidential. But you cannot expect your spouse to anticipate some of the more bizarre consequences of an unguarded comment, for example, a comment innocently made to an old friend or relative living thousands of miles away.

The disastrous consequences of one inadvertent comment are worth citing here. A minister's husband mentioned something about her search to a geographically distant relative, only to discover that her relative did not keep the confidence. (And why would her relative recognize how important the confidence was?) The relative, remembering someone who lives in the town where the minister was candidating, called a friend who called another friend, this person being a member of the prospective congregation. The cat was out of the bag, not only embarrassing the candidate and the search committee but jeopardizing the candidacy as well. Worse yet, as the name of the candidate and her current setting spread in the prospective congregation, a member of the prospective church called the candidate's current church, letting a member of the minister's current congregation know that the minister was about to leave.

While nightmarish, it is not a far-fetched story. Many stories I have heard are even more unlikely than this one. It is imperative for your spouse to understand the need for confidentiality. The last thing you want or need is tension between you and your significant other because your possible new call was jeopardized by his or her speaking too freely.

- Just as you need close, confidential relationships in which you can get support, perspective, and advice during a search, so does your spouse.

Be sure to provide the support your spouse or life partner needs to seek out a confidential relationship of his or her own, for example, with a therapist or spiritual director if he or she so desires.

CHAPTER 6

Who Am I?
Preparing to Be a Candidate

O ne minister, in the course of four years, moved from church A to church B to church C. Churches B and C were two of the largest and most prestigious churches in his denomination in the country. What is remarkable is that he did this without completing an official, up-to-date profile. Here's how it happened.

The first call was occasioned by the "old boy network." Because of the prestige of the man making the reference, congregation B thought the candidate to be of high enough quality that they would not need an up-to-date accounting of his ministry in church A. Unfortunately, when he arrived at church B, the information congregation B had disclosed about themselves had also been less than complete.

Having served at church B only three years (perhaps long enough for Jesus, but not for most of us!), the minister received a phone call from a member of church C, another large, geographically distant congregation in the midst of a search. It seems that this member of church C had been talking with a friend from church A and mentioned that congregation C was looking for a new minister. The friend from church A (who knew that the minister was having a rough go of it at church B) gave the minister's name to the person from church C, who promptly phoned the minister directly (even though she was not on church C's search committee). She then phoned the chair of the search committee and was (quite properly!) strenuously chastised for interfering. The minister avoided updating his profile this second time by pointing out the obvious: that he was not actively looking and thus could not provide an updated profile. The minister wrote a long letter, personalized for the particular mission of church C, and after an interview received the call.

Preparing Our Papers

Of course, most of us will not find ourselves in such a situation. We will likely have to update our profiles before we become active candidates. Ministers I have interviewed report a wide range of experiences with this activity. One said that the form is "incredibly tedious and takes forever to prepare," and that, even now, the denomination is "preparing to make it more time consuming and arcane." Another said that "it was very easy for the profile to be put together" and that few issues came up when he revised his profile.

Regardless of one's attitude toward the task, the uniformity of the profile form allows committees to standardize their methods of evaluation. The form is intended to make the process fair.

Completing the profile will often raise a number of issues, listed below as specific suggestions:

- Consider keeping a journal while you are putting together your profile. You may be surprised at the feelings that come to the surface as you summarize your accomplishments and articulate your credo. A journal may also be helpful when you are interviewing.

- One of the major blocks that prevent ministers from initiating their profiles is lack of practice at focusing on their own lives and feelings. Keeping a journal provides an opportunity to do this without the pressure that accompanies writing a profile. And when it comes time to write the essay portions of your profile, a journal will help you overcome the inertia that often plagues ministers in the profile process.

- Give yourself at least two weeks, and perhaps a month, to work on your denomination's forms. By resigning yourself to the fact that this is an ongoing project, you will likely have more thoughts and recall more accomplishments than you would if you rushed through the process.

- Keep a record of your professional accomplishments and achievements, including initiatives you have led in your congregation. Looking back at annual reports or recent evaluations often provides such a record. Because annual evaluations are all too rare in our profession, assembling such a record is a crucial preliminary step in preparing your profile. And, it will make you feel good about your ministry. It will also help you guard against any tendency to exaggerate.

- Don't exaggerate. Write about the things you have actually accomplished and feel good about rather than rationalize what you almost did or wished you had done.
- Don't plagiarize. Senator Joe Biden was not the first to have his ambition dashed because he lost sight of the difference between quoting and appropriating the work of another. If you get frustrated or run short on time, try to remember that the best thing about your thoughts and words is that they are yours. If you give that up, you sacrifice your integrity.
- Don't use funds from your current church to make yourself more marketable in the eyes of a potential church. Ministers have been known to publish a church brochure that emphasized their credentials or take out large advertisements in the local newspaper with their picture prominently displayed.[1] Obviously, this is tacky. And besides, most of the time, what you have done will be obvious to a search committee.
- Be honest.

Honesty

It is important here to delve a little deeper into the topic of being honest in preparing our papers. The question of honesty brings up the question of authenticity, a central issue in our ministries and in our relationships with God. While we would all prefer to keep our flaws to ourselves, search committees are in the business of discovering them. An interview can elevate a single quality to a position of decisive importance, even when it is not a flaw. Thus, we may choose not to mention in our papers, or in the interview, a particular characteristic or quality that could become a red herring, but if we don't mention it as a candidate and we are called, what will happen when the congregation finds out?

Gay and lesbian ministers experience this dilemma in a profound way. When determining what to reveal and what not to reveal, theirs is a particularly difficult challenge.

Emory Griffin urges us to be transparent in both our preaching and congregational interactions in his essay entitled "Self-Disclosure": "There's no better way of building trust with a new congregation than through self-disclosure."[2] But what is at stake in writing our profiles is different from what is at stake in preaching to a congregation where we are well established. Once we are part of a congregation, we try to promote an atmosphere of trust and openness. Becoming part of that congregation, however, involves judgment. Of course, judgment and trust do not necessarily conflict. But in the real world, it is often the case that a vociferous member of a committee will judge as unacceptable an aspect of our beliefs or past activity that is peripheral to who we are and how we will minister in that setting. By including it in our profiles, our candidacies may be scuttled.

On the other hand, deciding to exclude something significant from our written profiles with the intention of commenting on it during the interview may have merit. Worth noting are two ministers—both currently serving congregations—who have adopted this approach. Both ministers have impressive profiles—so impressive, in fact, that one has had 35 interviews and the other 24 interviews (and 16 visits to hear her preach). Both of these ministers are gay. Sadly, neither has received a new call.

While it is up to us to determine what we will share, disclose, and emphasize in writing our profiles, we have no control over how members of a search committee will respond. Thus, we must intentionally examine what our searches are about. If we understand our callings to require full self-disclosure, then a search should be directed at finding a congregation that wants to call us, warts and all. If, on the other hand, we choose a more gradual approach to self-disclosure, then our search should focus on finding a congregation that will grow in acceptance of us.

Preparing Our Souls

You can only be effective with your strengths, not your weaknesses.
Peter Drucker, *Reflections of the Lamp 3*[3]

Profiles often take weeks to prepare, and the process confronts us again and again with the brutal fact that we are actively considering a change. The process itself is very strenuous. It stresses us in both obvious and subtle ways. While some may try to negotiate the process on their own, we would do well to acknowledge our need for spiritual support early on. By calling upon the Holy Spirit we acknowledge our need for strength beyond what we can muster for ourselves. And with the help of the Holy Spirit we prepare ourselves for new and unfamiliar tests.

Several of the ministers interviewed for this book indicated that the search process raised in them many of the same feelings they had in junior high school when they first began dating. They were uneasy about whether or not they would be liked by the search committee. They worried that after half an hour they would know this was not the church for them but would have to go through with the visit just the same. Still, these same ministers vowed that they experienced the presence of the Holy Spirit in the process.

Any attempt to characterize exactly how the Holy Spirit is manifest during this process would be ill-considered. Ministers and search committees are all over the map when it comes to ascribing both positive and negative influence to the Holy Spirit.

I know a minister who, having been asked to interview at 24 churches without receiving a call, reports feeling that God was playing dirty tricks on her, that the Holy Spirit had been "thwarted" in the search process, that God was incarnated in the active support she received from friends, and that she felt more clear about her sense of call than ever before. In the end, she said, "I can't imagine doing anything other than being a minister."

Another minister described his experience with three churches in this way: "First, a black church in Brooklyn sent me its profile. After a few days of thinking about it, I wondered, 'Could this be God's will?' Other church profiles I had easily thrown away, but this one had to be taken seriously. Then another church kept pushing itself on me. I thought it was a complete mismatch, but they thought I was a perfect fit (even though I did not fit their expressed criteria). Finally, another church, of which I was only dimly aware, was looking for a new minister. A friend of mine was asked by someone on the search committee if she knew of anyone. She gave my name and two months later I accepted a call."

While all ministers agree that the Holy Spirit is involved, that involvement may be incarnated in discussions with friends, family, and search committees, or through prayer and human agency. It seems the effects of its involvement cannot in any way be known in advance or controlled. What can be known in advance and controlled is our openness and receptivity to whatever the Holy Spirit may do with us, our loved ones, our ministries, and our futures. Maintaining that openness is the work of prayer. Prayer never diminishes the importance of our well-honed skills of discernment yet always seeks to subordinate any of the hunches, inclinations, or notions we may have to the presence of the Holy Spirit.

Beyond Gifts Identification

Many of us are the last to recognize those strengths we bring to ministry. Taking an inventory of our gifts not only will prepare our responses to interview questions, but will prepare our souls for the process.[4] By reminding ourselves of the armor God has given us in the form of specific gifts and talents, we will not soon forget that we are children of God and are called by God to undertake marvelous and difficult challenges.

Many books urge us to clarify our direction and articulate our dream as an essential part of preparation.[5] Although this is an important ingredient and a necessary first step if we are to overcome inertia and actually begin the search process, it is equally important that we not cling too tightly to our specific, original articulation of that dream. Only we can identify the nature of the ministry we are seeking, but we must be open to the myriad ways in which God's desires will become manifest in the process. For most of us, the period between our first inclination to launch a search and our acceptance of a call is two to four years. During this time, our understanding of direction can and likely will change many times.

We should be particularly suspicious of our dreams and desires if there is a tight correlation between the direction in which we feel God is calling us and the values our culture ubiquitously promulgates. In other words, we must closely examine whether we have equated ambition with "success." For example, if we are currently serving a church with average worship attendance of 100 and we feel certain that God is calling us to be senior minister of the next mega-church, we need to review the gap between reality and dream, and then examine why there is such a gap. Occasionally ministers (and others) travel the full distance from so-called humble beginnings to mountaintops.[6] Some of us will go that full distance, too. More often than not, however, such a gap is an indication of unexamined and misplaced ambition.

The time to undertake an examination is now, before we write our profiles. It is not enough to inventory our gifts only. We must also step back and ask what our findings represent. Gaining that perspective is best done in prayerful dialogue with God. What we discover in prayer may be hard to take. But if we fail to gain an honest perspective as we prepare our profiles, we will likely gain that perspective during the search process. It will come when members of a search committee consult the Holy Spirit and decide for themselves whether we are prepared for the course we have set for ourselves. While their decision may be exactly what we need to hear, better to make that determination in consultation with our Maker only, rather than subject ourselves to human judges whose response may be less than compassionate.

Taming Our Fantasies

As we increase our efforts on behalf of a new call, we can become prone to daydreams and fantasies that can break our concentration and erode our focus, decreasing our effectiveness as a minister. While these invasions usually catch us by surprise, they are often associated with the long-term nature and future events of our current work. For example, finding the energy to stay focused on drafting the church activities calendar for next year may become difficult. We may resist the request to schedule yet another special meeting to design the church planning retreat. We may lack enthusiasm when the new moderator (whom we worked so hard to have nominated, and whose candidacy broke all the molds) comes to us wanting to start a two-year project that will enable the congregation to discover and define its guiding mission.

Amidst these difficulties with focus and long-term commitment, we are distracted by fantasies of a different setting, different people, different challenges. We imagine ourselves ministering in situations that before we had only envied. Fantasy is a much more pleasant place to dwell than the realities of our current setting, particularly when something in the current setting is not going well, a situation that leads most of us to initiate a change.

Don't think it won't happen! The challenge is to be prepared for it. As we initiate the search process, we need to visit and revisit our current (immediate) understanding of our callings. Our understanding will evolve as we negotiate the gap between our current reality and our sense of God's pull to something different. While we cannot eliminate or prematurely resolve the challenge, we can serve God by praying for guidance.

Simultaneous Insider and Outsider

Parish ministry asks a great deal of clergy. Most of us oblige by giving to our congregations all, or at least most, of our professional identity. Many of us identify ourselves so much with the ups and downs of our congregations that our spiritual identity is tied more closely to our congregations than to anything else.

For example, praise for a sermon, conflict in a committee, or a dispute among staff can have an enormous impact on our spiritual lives. In fact, these disturbances can outweigh and even counteract the impact of our daily prayers. Indeed, many of us merge our prayer lives into our professional lives so thoroughly that our prayers are largely prompted by, and often are responses to, the lives of our parishes. Thus, our prayer lives are often reduced to prayers of lament, celebration, or petition on behalf of others. What we need is to know who we are with God apart from our congregations and our roles as ministers. Only then will we have a genuine spiritual identity to bring to our work.

All of this shifts when we begin our search process, and our gaze, once reserved exclusively for our congregations, is divided. We remain fully involved in and concerned about the ongoing challenges of our current congregations. Yet we are also drawn to another place, not yet identified, where we at least hope to live out the next stage of our callings.

The impact of this shift on our relationship with our current congregations is significant. Most of us are deeply invested in a wide variety of decisions and outcomes in our current congregations for two reasons: First, we believe these directions are the best outcome for the congregation. Second, they represent our own personal preferences.

When we initiate a search, these two motives suddenly distinguish themselves from one another. We may find that our willingness to "go the extra mile" on any number of issues wanes. Consider the attitudes of this minister before and after his search:

Before the search is initiated	After the search is initiated
"Although it will take a great deal of my time, and many in the congregation will resist or even oppose it, that capital campaign is essential to the future of our church. We have to make it happen."	"If these people can't see the obvious reality that they need to conduct a capital campaign, I'm not going to force it on them. In the end, it has to be their decision."
"What she said about last week's sermon was right. This week I'm going to turn over a new leaf and take my preparation for sermons more seriously."	"All they ever do is criticize. I've been told countless times how good my sermons are. Maybe they'll be more appreciated in another church."
"I need to create a better system for visitation. It's crucial that I make the time to see those people who are sick and in the hospital, in addition to seeing others from time to time."	"All things being equal, I would visit all those people, just as I used to. But things aren't equal. I have to get this profile done and I have to finish those letters of interest to various conference ministers."

Prior to initiating a search, we had an unalloyed commitment to our current congregations. Our own self-interests were usually aligned with, or at least subordinate to—rarely in conflict with—the interests of our congregations. Now a new factor is introduced. A new set of self-interests now cause us to recalculate our positions on any number of issues. We have become a simultaneous insider and outsider.

For Your Reflection

- While we'll never have the chance to go back and do it all over again, as we plan for the future, it is good to learn from the past. Looking back at your present ministry, can you identify any situations where, in the beginning, you were less than forthcoming about yourself, your family, or your beliefs? Was your ministry significantly compromised because of it? This exercise will guide you in making decisions about what to include in your profile and what to discuss in an interview.

- What are your true motives in pursuing a new call? To what extent are your motives shaped by God, and to what extent do they grow out of the values promulgated by our culture? Have soul searching and prayer given you confidence in answering these questions?
- Develop an outline of the projects and initiatives you anticipate in your current congregation over the next three to four years. Could some be accurately described as "pet projects," that is, are any unnecessary for your congregation to flourish?
- Now is the time to decide how to best use your energy for the good of your current congregation. Once you have begun the search process, that energy will likely decrease. Since your congregants will not be able to help you (because they will not know you are searching), you must create your own triage system to assure that your energy goes where it is most needed.

CHAPTER 7

A (Second) Full-Time Job: Being an Active Candidate

Perhaps this chapter's title overstates the point. After all, in the secular world, two-thirds of all people seeking a new job spend less than five hours a week on their searches.[1] But clergy are different. Like our secular colleagues, we must jump through all sorts of hoops, including filling out forms, writing letters and follow-up letters, making calls, arranging for interviews, and so forth. But clergy must also set aside sufficient time to reflect on, anticipate, and respond to the conflicts, pitfalls, dilemmas and challenges presented by the process, many of which manifest themselves in one or another form of increased anxiety within the congregation and its leadership. This chapter explores such conflicts, dilemmas, and challenges, for which few guidelines currently exist.[2]

Setting Boundaries

Many of us have not mastered the spiritual art of setting boundaries. We feel as though we have to be available at all times to any congregant or community member who might need us. While this is often linked with a certain psychological orientation that may bear examination, it is frequently a spiritual issue, showing a lack of confidence in God's omnipresence or a misplaced confidence in our own presence, that is, considering ourselves indispensable.

Once we become involved in a search, setting boundaries becomes essential. The search process will require us to devote time to the many tasks of a search, thus rendering us less available to our current congregations. Because many of those tasks are covert, and few of us are accustomed to the mind-set required to live a double life, we shall have to develop new habits, new responses to certain questions, and new criteria by which to plan.

Absence and Travel

One unique aspect of the ministry is that everyone in the profession is occupied at almost exactly the same time each week. When it comes to the search process, this means that a search committee will likely want to interview us during the weekend, which will probably include preaching in a neutral pulpit on Sunday morning.

Many ministers do not serve with an ordained colleague in their congregation. Thus, we have no one who can substitute for us during unplanned absences. While senior ministers of large churches have more options, their schedules are often too cluttered to take an unplanned, three-day absence without a lot of explaining.

To avoid the problems occasioned by emergency arrangements, it is important to do some advanced planning. The best alternative is to look at each prospective church and identify how far along it is in its process. This may provide a rough idea when they may be interviewing. We can then plan our calendars so that we will have some flexibility to be absent one or two weekends in a two- or three-month period. It is much easier to cancel a scheduled absence on the third Sunday of next month than it is to explain to our director of Christian Education why we will have to miss Christian Education Sunday, which is only three weeks away.

Of course, even the most detailed planning offers no guarantee that a particular date will work both for us and for the search committee. Nevertheless, introducing some judicious planning will only ease the process.

Privacy

While most of us do a fine job protecting the confidentiality of others, we ministers rarely extend that protection to our own lives. Our lives, and the lives of our families, are frequently viewed by our congregants as an open book. This becomes all the more apparent when we engage in a search that requires us to communicate personal business in a private fashion. Because church members are often "nosey," we need to consider in advance the ways we can handle communication with prospective churches, without inviting questions from colleagues or congregants.

We will likely need to use a fax machine, copy machine, and computer during the search process. Typically, these resources are available for public or staff use. That being the case, we would be wise to plan ahead our use of these resources, particularly if they are located in a high-traffic area of the church office.

Likewise, use of the telephone merits forethought. Specifically, consider location:

- Where can we speak freely on a phone?
- Can a search committee member call us directly without going through a secretary?
- When we speak on the office phone, can we be heard by others?

In most cases, we will have to direct search-related calls to our homes. The home environment, however, leads to another set of concerns. Are there constraints to us using our home phones for professional business? Are our children used to this? Even if they understand that our conversations are normally confidential, how will they react to hearing a discussion about moving to another community? If they suspect something, they may not immediately discuss it with us. More likely, they'll talk it over with a friend at school or Sunday School.

Finally, the time will come in the search process when we will have to let a prospective church know how to reach us by phone. By addressing these concerns ahead of time, we will be able to provide a prospective church with access to us and still maintain our privacy.

The Interview

Interviewing is a multifaceted subject, well covered by many sources.[3] Therefore, here we will review a limited number of areas where the potential for conflict or spiritual distress is high, and particular topics not often discussed.

Prepare

One day, out of the blue, a phone call will come from a search committee. Our response, which will be critical in determining whether or not we remain a candidate, will depend on our preparedness.

A wise saying in the marshal art of Aikido is, "Expect nothing. Be ready for everything." Again and again, it seems that a search committee first contacts us at the worst possible time. No doubt, certain times can be inopportune. But if we are diligent in accepting God's guidance of and presence in the process, we will be ready. While I do not subscribe to the view that there is a reason for everything, I do believe that God is always available to us. In the case of a search, God is present as a resource in the process, both for us and for the committee.

God's presence is most readily accessed when, in our daily prayer life, we "prime the pump." We need to revisit, again and again, the reason we are doing all of this. We need to remind ourselves of the spiritual struggle that led us to this point. We need to bring before God our fears, insecurities, emptiness, and ambivalence. Acknowledging these truthfully before God will strengthen us for the moment we await.

Rehearse

Beyond the obvious strategic value of rehearsal, rehearsing will increase the likelihood that our answers and our composure will accurately reflect who we are to the committee. While few of us are capable of changing our entire identity in response to our circumstances, most of us are well versed at saying the appropriate thing at the right time to a particular person. Part of "picking our battles" in our current church is choosing to back off from a particular issue with one person, knowing that the time will come (say, at a department meeting) for us to take our stand. This is just one aspect of effective leadership.

Integrity is another. To maintain our integrity amidst the search process, we must begin with the end in mind. During Gandhi's lifetime, many observed that he contradicted himself on countless occasions. Of course, his consistent response was that he cared not at all about consistency. Rather, he believed that what mattered was maintaining the purity of his means. In so doing he would guarantee the purity of the ends, even when they appeared inconsistent.

We maintain our integrity in the search process through a similar approach. While we may be able to "justify" or "rationalize" offering a committee the responses we believe they want to hear, doing so will bring us no closer to an authentic call. Rehearsing forces us to identify the core values that motivate our ministries. If we are to be chosen, it should be on those grounds—not because we are capable of providing the "right" answers to the committee.

After all, in finding a new call, we do not want to bring with us the shackles fitted at our former congregation at times when we compromised too much of what we believed in or stood for. The point of heeding a new call is to find a congregation that freely desires a minister with the gifts and call we have to offer when we act in concordance with our understanding of God's will. The best way to ensure a meaningful outcome is to rehearse how we can best articulate such an understanding of ourselves.

Identify Bottom Lines

Because ministry deals with issues of the most personal and spiritual nature, each of us is likely to be inflexible on a few issues central to our understanding of discipleship. Because God created a world in which we are blessed with freedom, these issues vary enormously from person to person, from congregation to congregation, and from culture to culture.

We should first attempt to identify these issues when we write our profiles. We may choose not to reveal them on our profiles, but instead want to discuss them at the interview. Or, we may choose to remain silent about an issue altogether. Among the personal issues that could appear on a particular minister's list: divorce, disability, dyslexia, alcoholism, and so on.

Issues beyond the personal, however, those ideals we hold so strongly that it would be impossible for us to minister in a context that did not support them—these constitute our bottom lines. Some possible "bottom line" issues: ministerial identity as "preacher and teacher," use of inclusive language (which could take the form of refusing to pick noninclusive hymns), theological opposition to serving a church with an endowment, commitment to pacifism, willingness to serve only an "open and affirming" church (that is, a congregation that welcomes and accepts gays and lesbians as full members of the body of Christ), refusal to allow associates to baptize in the name of anything other than the "Father, Son, and Holy Spirit," and so on.

If we are at peace about our life's journey, and if we hold to our principles because they are a source of integrity and joy, then losing a position because a search committee deems this aspect of our identities incompatible will not be tragic. Such integration is hard to come by, though. Wounds are frequent. This is why it is so important to clarify for ourselves exactly what these issues are. While we don't want to be rejected for the wrong reason, we definitely don't want to be called under false pretenses.

Include Your Spouse

It used to be that when a church hired a minister, it could also count on his wife serving the church and her husband's ministry. Those days are over. Today's ministers don't have wives; we have spouses or significant others. And these adults have lives and careers of their own.

In choosing a minister, the search committee is also choosing his or her spouse and family. Most churches, with the possible exception of megachurches, resemble small towns. The personal lives of their moral and spiritual leaders will be scrutinized. Thus, marital and parental relationships can contribute either to a successful ministry or a failed one.

Virtually all search committees recognize that this is a touchy issue and avoid it as best they can. Yet by their comfort level and thoughtfulness toward our spouses, the search committee will provide clues about how the congregation as a whole may respond to our spouses should we accept a call. We need to be attentive in assessing a committee's attitude in this area.

Even if the committee avoids the issue, we should make sure that we address it. It is in our own interest, every bit as much as it is in a committee's interest, that our spouses be in on our decisions. Indeed, a recent article indicated that the happiness of the spouse is among the most important ingredients pastors cite in speaking about their success.[4] It is critical that our spouses not only be comfortable with the people and the environment of our prospective churches but that they embrace them.

Another reason to involve our spouses in the process is that the interview is inevitably a trying experience. Any twelve-on-one "discussion" would be. Having our spouses present in the room provides us with both support and an additional set of eyes and ears. This can be very useful after the interview, when we try to process what took place.

Keeping the Interview Private

The date we set for the interview will significantly influence the story we tell our current congregations about why we will not be present. An interview over a "long weekend" may allow excuses unavailable on normal weekends. Each situation is unique.

If we have children, we should give considerable thought to what we tell them and who will take care of them. Keep in mind that if there is any variation between what we tell our current congregations and what we tell our children, chances are that the discrepancy will be noticed. Curious parishioners often pry, and children may unintentionally reveal something that will raise questions. Creating an alibi, although extremely uncomfortable for many ministers and their spouses, may be necessary.

Of course, the fewer people we tell, the better.[5] No matter how effective the alibi, there will be people in our congregations who will sense that it's not the full story, and that it may not be a true story. Don't be surprised by this. These are intuitive souls who always seem to sense when something is up. If we're fortunate, these people will not be busybodies. If we're unfortunate, we may have some explaining to do.

Having taken all of this into account, we would do well to consider some form of the truth: "I was asked to preach at a church in Seattle where I have some friends, so my wife and I decided to spend a few extra days there." Even if this is a completely truthful statement, and it raises no further concerns, it also may have a peculiar effect. It may indirectly communicate that something is going on, beyond the issue of where we are spending the weekend. If this is the conclusion drawn, the long-range prospects for our ministries could be diminished out of ambiguity about the future. This constitutes a major dilemma.

Honesty Revisited

At some point in the process, we will need to be honest. It may be when we write our profiles, although this could be premature. It may be in an initial phone conversation, or at our first or second interview. Whenever we choose to remove the veil of privacy, it should be during the search process. We should not wait until we move to a new congregation. Remember, to be effective in our new congregations, our ministries must be rooted in authenticity.[6] What God will accomplish through an alliance with a new congregation begins with trust.

Our decision to trust the committee and to share openly will often prompt greater openness on their part too. These are moments of *kairos*—moments when God intrudes on the normal course of events, pushing aside the linear *chronos* of our clocks and replacing it with a moment in which time stops and God intrudes. Such moments are often awkward. A candidate may learn that, four years ago, the church treasurer embezzled funds, or the committee may be surprised to hear a candidate expand on a cryptic comment in his or her profile. These moments are born in revelation and beg for resolution. Suddenly, both candidate and committee realize that the dance they are doing may be for keeps. In a flash of honest disclosure, trust is tested. How the candidate and committee respond can determine the extent to which trust takes root. These intense moments are the ones usually remembered by both candidate and committee.

We must remember that the search process forces both a candidate and the search committee to condense into only a few hours enough exposure and meaning to make a decision that will affect the life of every member of the church. The process is intense. It is necessary for both sides to open themselves so that trust may evolve quickly. Otherwise, little of merit will result.

As the ministers being interviewed, we have a good bit of control over this dimension of the interview. If we are forthcoming, open, and honest, the committee is likely to respond in kind when invited. If we can establish that atmosphere in a first or second interview, it is likely that we are well on our way to receiving a call.

Along the same lines, it is worth re-examining the issue of being open and honest with our current congregations. Having engaged in an active search, we are now responsible for a double trust (a double cross, if we're not careful!). As is always the case, as ministers, we must earn the trust of our congregations. If we choose to keep our active searches secret, this double life is a reality with which we will have to make peace. And part of that reality is an obligation not to alarm our current congregations by providing them with a reason to doubt our trustworthiness. We need to be grounded in the recognition that what we are doing is properly sanctioned as part of the course of normal events: a minister considering a new call.

The Visit

Consider these two stories:

It's Sunday morning. You get a brief phone call at home two hours before worship begins. It's an awkward conversation, not only for you but for the caller as well. This person seems surprised to get you on the phone, yet she knows your name. She wants to know when worship begins and when it is likely to end. After you hang up, you realize that she may have thought she was phoning the church. An odd confusion. You make a note to call the phone book company to see if the phone numbers are switched.

Later that morning at church, twenty minutes before worship, a visitor comes to the church office asking to use the phone. She says that she's from a well-known city 800 miles away and has to get a plane back. None of this is unusual, since your church is located in a major city and you receive visitors all the time.

That afternoon, it occurs to you that the major city she was returning to is the airport hub for the town where you are a candidate. Suddenly you realize that she was also the same person who had phoned you at home. She must be on the search committee! She had simply mixed up the phone numbers, thinking that she was calling the church and would receive an answering machine with the information she needed. Good thing that everything went fine at worship!

True story.

Two members of the search committee fly in to hear you on Pentecost Sunday. They arrive the evening before, and because of their tight schedule they suggest that they meet with you Saturday night at 8:30 p.m. A storm delays them and they arrive at 10:30 p.m. They ask you to visit with them while they get a bite to eat. Although you are an early riser, you agree. They keep you up well past midnight.

After worship the next day, they ask to come over to your home for a brief conversation. Just as you finish picking up the mess in the living room, they arrive. Following brief introductions, your wife arranges for the children to be out of earshot (they know nothing of your search). When your guests leave an hour and a half later, you wonder if you passed the marathon test.

Also a true story.

What if a headhunter came to the home of a lawyer for a surprise interview when that home is owned by her boss—who happens to live next door? It's almost impossible to imagine! Yet such practical and relational complexity is the stuff ministerial searches are made of.

The sequence of events in both the preceding stories happened to the same minister, except that all three visitors came from a single congregation. As nerve-wracking as these situations sound, they are mild compared with the following:

> Two men showed up in church one day, asked to see me following the service and informed me that God had sent them and that I was to be their new pastor. When I told them as politely as I could that I had no such communication from God, they suggested that I at least fly to their city, meet with the committee and talk further about the opportunity. Since I had had a preaching mission in that church a few years earlier, I felt I already knew all I needed to know about the church and respectfully declined.[7]

Before we find ourselves in a surprising and awkward situation, some self-examination is in order. How should we respond when surprised? How strong is our need to be in control? How do we experience the Holy Spirit? Do we regard such encounters as God's "dirty tricks," or are they playful gestures? Or, do they have nothing to do with God?

Avoiding Breaches in Confidentiality

We must make it absolutely clear to any committees with whom we have contact that they could significantly undermine and jeopardize the future of our current ministries if they violate the normal paths of confidential inquiry. Remember, committee members are not necessarily experienced at searches. They could naively phone the president or moderator (who may know nothing of our explorations) of our current congregations, or they might clumsily phone us at the office and leave their name and number, indicating that the purpose of the call concerns the search committee of some church in a distant town. We cannot expect them to anticipate every effect their actions may have on us.

We can, however, ask committee members to let us know a day before they plan to contact our references. We can then take the time to phone each of our references first. At each contact, we should remind them of the importance of confidentiality. We should update them about our discussions with a particular congregation. And, we should thank them for their time and support and for keeping our confidence.

We may not be able to anticipate effectively all the possible ways in which confidentiality can be breached, but we can be vigilant with our intentions and in our prayers.

Juggling Possibilities

The complexity of our circumstances increases exponentially when we are an active candidate in several congregations at the same time. Talented ministers engaged in a search have told me stories of discovering representatives from two or even three churches in the back pews of their current churches. As previously noted, search committee "scouts" often arrive unannounced, and if they have traveled far, they are likely to bring with them expectations for our time, particularly following worship.

Another enormously complex task is remembering what we have told each congregation. Through phone conversations, interviews at the prospective church, and scouting visits to our current churches, a lot of ground will be covered. When simultaneously in contact with several search committees, it is both predictable and appropriate that we emphasize different aspects of our ministries and share a variety of stories to illustrate our gifts and approaches. It is always embarrassing when someone repeats a story they don't remember telling at a previous encounter. As a candidate, this can happen easily. The point here is not to limit ourselves to a few canned stories we make sure to cover with each church on a first interview; the point is to anticipate this problem before we become seriously engaged with a second or third potential placement. As previously noted, keeping notes after each conversation is one way to address this concern.

In addition to the issue of monitoring what we have told each committee, it often happens that the various committees are slow to progress, from our point of view. We may be a highly placed candidate at what we perceive would be an ideal call, only to receive a firm offer from a church that interests us far less. In these circumstances, there are no rules or guidelines. Making lists of the positive and negative features of each call offered may be helpful in sizing up a potential position, but no list can resolve the existential reality we must face: that our destiny, our call, becomes more and more defined as we choose one path over another. We are not passive passengers on a bus driven by God. Our character, our prayer lives, and our discernment come together to influence our decision making. Through those decisions we co-author our lives with our God.

Can a minister sincerely juggle simultaneous possible calls? So long as we are clear that our search is primarily a journey of listening to God and considering the opportunities placed before us, we can. If the complexity and intensity of the final stages of our search distract us from the critical spiritual resources at our command, however, and we determine our decisions using only some form of cost-benefit analysis, then it is quite possible that our decision making will be indistinguishable from that of a person whose search proceeds without the benefit of discernment. We must take the time to reflect on our calls. Our freedom of choice, as well as the sincerity of exercising that freedom, is underwritten by our connectedness with God through prayer and discernment. If we maintain the connection, we can sincerely juggle our options, because we are sincerely searching for the direction in which God will lead us. If we lose the connection with God or allow our discipline to lapse, our future is likely to be as hollow as our decision.

For Your Reflection

- Review the section earlier in this chapter on privacy. Based on the questions regarding your availability over the telephone at your church and at home, review your behavior and shape some policies that will govern your search-related telephone communication.
- Reflect on the issue of boundaries. Try to anticipate the way your overall attitude toward boundaries may expose you to difficult situations as your search unfolds.

- Part of any search is spiritual preparation. Unfortunately, just when you have less time available because you are interacting with committees, you need to set aside still more time for disciplined prayer. Examine your prayer life. Be sure to take whatever time you need to bring before God the many concerns raised by your search.

- Before interviewing, peruse some of the excellent material on writing a personal mission statement, for example, Stephen R. Covey's *The Seven Habits of Highly Effective People.* By working through some of the exercises, you will undoubtedly come to understand more clearly your gifts, your call, and those areas that are most important to you. The process may even put you in touch with the most important sources of joy in your life.

- Look back to the time when you began your current position. Focus on the challenges and difficulties you faced in the first year or two. Was any of that friction occasioned by your decision to withhold personal information from the search committee or the congregation? Looking back, was the price you paid for withholding the information worth it? How might this shape your current decision to be forthcoming with a committee?

CHAPTER 8

The Call

Waiting

Waiting for God's call is one of the most spiritually challenging activities in the life of a minister. While much of our effort in our congregations is an expression of our attempts to be instruments of God, waiting for God's call forces us to acknowledge that there is only so much we can do. Once we have addressed all possibilities to advance the search process, we must wait.

Some lessons are available in the midst of this waiting, lessons that can enlarge our relationships with God, enhance our understanding of ourselves, and empower us with compassion for others who are forced to wait. Learning to offer our anxious hearts to God is among the most important of these lessons. The peace of God, which surpasses all understanding (Phil. 4:7), is not something we achieve by accomplishing all of our to-dos. It is a gift God graciously bestows upon those who seek a transformation from anxiety to rest.

As long as we convince ourselves that we are in control of our ministry and its influence, we cannot learn this lesson. In fact, we may need to be rendered "out of control," which aptly describes how we feel when we have heard nothing from a committee in the two months since a promising interview. Facing such a circumstance, we must learn to recognize that there is nothing more we can do to hasten an outcome. Rather, we must look anew to discover God's presence in the midst of our quiet desperation. The strength available to us when we tap into this resource can not only enhance our own lives, it can expand our ability to minister to others who face similar circumstances.

Loren Mead writes about the impatience some ministers experience while waiting for a call. The period of waiting sometimes unmasks attitudes that would otherwise remain hidden. For example, the impatience of some ministers is related to their view that congregations without settled (as opposed to interim) ministers are incapable of real ministry.

> The impatience of the clergy often masks a kind of imperial concept of ministry—that there really isn't any ministry in the congregation until they have a clergy person there. Most who are impatient with the wait do not believe in an imperial ministry of the clergy with their conscious minds, but this may be a relic of a concept they need to move beyond. Or at least examine.[1]

Finally, we must remember that while we are waiting to see the signs of God's activity that may take us in a new direction, we are still called to minister to our current congregations. Mead offers a very helpful table,[2] part of which is summarized below, listing suggestions about how we should respond to certain events in the search process.

When. . .	What To Do
All is going well and you feel good about what you are doing	Pay attention to your job and find ways to do it better.
All is well, but you wonder if you have stayed long enough	Pay attention to your job.
You decide you should seek another position	Be sure to keep your current job on track by doing your job.
You get a nibble or inquiry	Pay attention to your own job and people.
The nibble becomes courtship	Pay more attention to your current job and people.
A call is extended	Pay careful attention to your current job and people.
A call is not extended	Pay special attention to your current job.
You get turned down and feel discouraged	Pay attention to your current job.

We should take to heart Mead's connection between our best interests and serving our current churches. He has decades of experience with the matter. His insistence that we continue to do our current jobs is a testimony to the difficulty of serving two masters.

Considering

Although few ministers have more than a dim memory of how horrible it felt to be rejected for a position we coveted, most of us have a vivid recollection of the phone call offering us a position we ultimately accepted. It is a moment that has long been anticipated, the fulfillment of months of prayer and work.

Our Work Is Not Over: Buying Time

When a call is extended to us, we have a decision to make. Having done everything possible to get to this position, having done everything in our power to hasten the day that we would receive this phone call, we now must slow everything down. We need time to consider such an important decision.

Until now, the committee has been in control of most of the process. It has, for the most part, determined the pace. But the moment we receive that phone call, the power shifts. With an offer on the table, before we sign on the dotted line, we have as much power as we will ever have in the process. We become a full partner in determining the pace and direction of what unfolds.

Many candidates find this shift awkward. Indeed, it is a challenge to receive this new freedom gracefully. We would be wise to consider viewing our response to this phone call as perhaps the first exercise of our ministerial authority at what might become our new congregations.[3] As in so many circumstances where ministry is exercised, the situation can be complicated. Here, complications can increase because we are an interested party.

How much time to buy may vary from situation to situation. It is reasonable to ask for a week, but if the committee resists, compromise is usually an option. Five days, four days, three days—try to negotiate enough time to consider the call.

Expressing Gratitude

Expressing genuine gratitude is of primary importance. This can be done in many ways, but it cannot and must not be faked. Although we have waited a long time for this moment and may have agonized greatly in the process, the committee has worked tirelessly to arrive at this conclusion. While we may view the committee's call merely as a re-engagement of an offer we had abandoned all hope of receiving, the committee has been steadily progressing toward selecting us as the next minister. In such a case, will we be able to express our gratitude at the drop of a hat? It's a question worthy of reflection.

I know of one situation in which the call came while the candidate and his family were vacationing with the head of his current church's diaconate. It was an idyllic week. The two families had a close friendship—husbands, wives, and children. The call came. There was one phone. It was in the kitchen and had a short cord. The call came while everyone was busy in the kitchen cleaning up after supper. Luckily, the host was also a reference, so he knew this day was coming. The candidate minister had given the phone number to a committee member in case the committee reached a decision while he was away. Nevertheless, when the call came, the experience was overwhelming.

In a flash, the minister knew that the contentment he had felt during the course of his ten-year ministry would be exchanged for new challenges and opportunities. On the phone was the jubilant, excited committee. The whole committee was on speakerphone, eagerly awaiting his immediate, positive response. Blissfully washing dishes were the minister's family and their best friends. Even if tinged with nostalgia, gratitude was clearly the appropriate response. Explaining the unusual circumstances in rather muffled tones, the minister did his best to express his excitement and gratitude.

Balancing: It's Not an Act

When Jesus admonished the disciples to be "wise as serpents, gentle as doves," he emphasized the importance of discovering the kind of balance many of us find elusive. We all know people with serpentlike instincts when it comes to negotiating. We also know wonderful people who can't get to first base in a negotiation. We must seek to be both wise and gentle.

Rector and author Douglas Scott says that "accepting a call is at best a series of tradeoffs."[4] On the one hand, we have to be pragmatic utilitarians. On the other, we want to go through this experience being as open as possible to all that God would teach us.

There are resources that detail questions to consider before entering into a negotiation.[5] What is critical in that consideration, however, is that, in addition to asking as many of the right questions as possible, we also pay close attention to the feelings that are driving our inclinations. If we are inclined to reject a position, we must push ourselves to articulate why. If we are overcome with joy or surprise over the fact that we are the committee's choice, we need to understand where that joy or surprise, and perhaps relief, are coming from. Without this level of self-understanding, we will be ineffective negotiators, hampered by ignorance of our own motivations.

Talking with others who are familiar with our circumstances can help. A spouse, for example, may be able to help us gain perspective on our feelings. Close friends who are familiar with our circumstances may be able to shed light on some of our doubts, suspicions, or fears. What we are after is a deeper understanding of our character, and how that character— as it has evolved over the years—is showing itself in response to this offer.

In addition to understanding why we are feeling what we are feeling, it is essential to seek God's guidance. With each rejection and with any offer, we are given a new opportunity to grow in our understanding of God's direction for our lives. That direction is not made manifest in the decision of a search committee to reject us or offer us a job. Rather, it is revealed through the understanding we acquire as we respond to whatever comes our way.[6]

Having clarified our feelings and consulted God's wisdom, it is time to become concrete in considering the call. We need to identify the issues associated with this new position, including the move, settling in, the new contract, and so on. It is important for us to examine our job experiences and identify the issues that have troubled us in previous positions. As we put this list together, consulting a spouse or life partner is always a good idea. Doing so will increase the likelihood that, in the heat of negotiation, his or her considerations will be factored in, too. Always keep in mind that in virtually every circumstance, it is acceptable to ask for more time to talk about some sticking point. Premature closure will help neither the congregation nor the candidate.

One final note: if you have not already done so, ask explicitly to speak with the treasurer at some point in the financial discussions. If the committee declines your request, make sure that its reason is convincing. Occasionally a committee moves ahead without authorization from the officers of the church. When this happens, the committee is negotiating under false pretenses—not a good way to start a new relationship!

Not Jumping to Accept a Call

An excellent student in her final year at a well-respected divinity school received three offers, each from a large church. She narrowed her choice to two, and during the week she requested to consider each call, she did all she could to evaluate her own needs, consider whether or not each setting could meet them, and get a better handle on what she might expect at each church. She knew that the most important predictor of an associate's happiness is the relationship between the associate and the senior minister, but she had been unable to contact the outgoing associate of the congregation she was favoring.

She had agreed to the committee's request for a 5:00 p.m. deadline on the last day of her week. At 4:45, while she and her husband were praying over the decision, the phone rang. It was the outgoing associate she had not yet reached. The associate told an unexpected story of conflict and woe. At 4:55 she phoned the other church and accepted their offer. Later she would say that God had intervened in the process. If we think it is a good idea to look into something before accepting a position, we should do everything in our power to complete our investigation.

On the other end of the spectrum is the minister who is completely discouraged after years of searching for a call and is finally offered a position. In such a situation, we would be wise not to jump at the call with untempered eagerness. Discernment in this situation is just as important as it is when three or four calls have been offered. As Richard Bolles warns, "Worse things can happen than not getting a call to an appropriate place, and getting a call to an inappropriate place is one of them."[7]

Accepting

Negotiating, Part 1

One of the great gifts of a new call is that, at least for a time, our lives are permeated with joy. Of course, that joy may be accompanied by fear and trembling, insecurity, exhaustion, relief, or any number of other emotions.

Some of our joy results from hard work and effective negotiating. If our negotiations have not been effective, if we have a lingering sense that we have been "had," then our joy will not likely be complete. In fact, our joy may be significantly tempered by bitterness or self-loathing—not a good way to begin a new ministry!

Amidst the ongoing excitement and overwhelming hope for new possibilities in our new positions, we must complete our negotiations. Beneath all the back-and-forth about benefits, vacation, study leave, the parsonage, salary, and so on, the two foundations of the agreement are clarity and authority.

Clarity is often abandoned in the rush of enthusiasm felt by both parties. Duration of vacation is one example. The terms of vacation may read "one month." But does this mean 30 days? 31 days? Four weeks (28 days)? A much more clear (and slightly more generous) description would be "five weeks, including Sundays."

Authority is less obvious. Through discrete inquiries, the candidate should gain an understanding of the relationship between the chair of the search committee (with whom negotiations normally take place) and the ongoing leadership of the church, especially the moderator or president, and the treasurer. As our focus shifts from search to ministry, the significance of the search committee will diminish, but the authority of the church governing body will remain. Occasionally there is a discrepancy between the search committee chair's understanding of what he or she is authorized to negotiate and the moderator's or president's expectations. Even if they see eye-to-eye, when the congregation votes on the candidate, they must also vote to accept terms of employment. It is in the interest of all parties that the terms negotiated are received favorably by the congregation.

While all of this may seem interminably complicated, especially when the discussions are transpiring over the phone or via e-mail, we should view this as an opportunity to improve our communication skills and set the stage for a ministry of clear communication. By effectively voicing the terms and successfully bringing all parties together in this agreement, we will have begun our ministry with an important precedent that will serve everyone well.

Negotiating, Part 2

Once an agreement on the terms of employment has been reached with the appropriate representatives of the congregation,[8] we, as candidates, must be cautious. Also note: if there is any reason to think that the congregation may reject the committee's choice, or that a split vote may occur, we would be wise to require that whatever we sign in advance be contingent not only upon an affirmative vote of the congregation but also our response to that vote. It would be a big mistake to sign an agreement to relocate our families contingent only on an affirmative vote of the congregation, and then later find out that the congregation split 60-40 to extend the call.

Another important issue to negotiate is how the search committee will notify the congregation of our acceptance. Typically they will circulate a brief biography or profile of who we are, our backgrounds, and limited information about our families. We should be involved in developing this circular. While we don't want to appear controlling, an inaccurate impression or a comment taken out of context can easily get blown out of proportion and featured in our dossier. Furthermore, very few committees will take adequate precautions to maintain confidentiality at this critical junction.

For a period of ten to twenty days, the new congregation will know something no one in our current congregations knows: that we are a candidate at a distant church and that we are about to leave. To reduce the likelihood that word will spread, and eventually reach our current congregations, we should insist that a separate, brightly colored insert be included with the circular warning all recipients of the need for strict confidentiality and pointing out that a new minister is not "called" until the congregation votes to "call" him or her.

Staying Involved

Accepted candidates enter into an unusual period at this point in the process. The time between when a final agreement is reached and when candidates go before their new congregations is often a month, rarely less than two weeks but sometimes as long as six. During this time, our current congregations will continue to need us. Festering disputes will flare, couples will approach us to officiate at their weddings several months away, new members will join, and plans for the youth mission to Nicaragua (only three months away!) will need to be finalized, including the purchase of nonrefundable tickets.

While it may be difficult to find the energy to stay involved with our current congregations during this special period, doing so will be fruitful. This is a time when we can gain new understanding about the interdependency of congregation and minister. While we may try to dodge the invitations and commitments for events beyond the event horizon of our move, we will plainly see just how essential a minister is to a congregation. We owe it to God and to the people God has given us for the past several years to stay involved in their lives, even though we know that our life will soon take another turn.

Keeping It to Ourselves

The agreement has been finalized and accepted. We're eagerly awaiting the start of a new call. Now we face up to six weeks of serving the congregation we will be leaving. Throughout this time, we will know something that those who depend upon us for leadership and spiritual guidance do not. In circumstance after circumstance, we feel we are betraying the trust of the people we have served and loved for years. And occasionally, that will be true.

Consider the following juxtaposition of emotions. On the one hand, we have just received affirmation of our ministerial gifts by the call of a congregation. On the other hand, daily we are forced to make excuses and even lie to members of our current churches.

If we are to survive this period of time with our emotional health intact, we must set aside time for prayer and quiet reflection. We need to stay in touch with our identity as children of God, an identity that is neither puffed up by affirmation nor undermined by deceit. If we fail, we will risk losing our sense of self just when we need it most.

Another way to maintain our emotional health during this time is confiding in our spouses or life partners. We will need to review our plans and discuss the sequence of events about to unfold, of course, but our spouses may also be able to help us deal with the enormous pressure we're under— pressure that has built up over the past many months (perhaps years) and has now shifted. Prior to finalizing our decision, the pressure was to continue to engage our current congregations while investigating new opportunities. Now the pressure is to hide our euphoric feelings and our sadness until we can let our current congregations know of our decision.

We and our spouses are embarking on an adventure. This is the time to remember our roots, to look back at our wedding vows and remember what we love most about each other. This is the time to reminisce about some of the most difficult times of the search process and count our blessings that we have found a new call. This is our time to regain the firm footing necessary in the coming months. This is not the time to phone our parents (or anyone else) to let them in on our plans.

A case in point: A Methodist minister was notified a month in advance of public notification that she would be going to her "dream" congregation. She made the mistake of telling a friend who lived halfway across the country, a friend who knew the information was not yet public and should be kept confidential. Her friend mentioned it to another friend, who knew someone in the town of the new congregation. It turns out that this friend, a man who had no involvement with this or any other church, happened to work for the local newspaper. Because he was unfamiliar with protocol, he published an announcement in the paper, one week before the denominational superintendent planned to notify the public. When the superintendent read the article in the newspaper, he almost canceled the move due to breach of confidentiality.

Few people can keep such important and exciting news secret for very long. This is yet another reason to use this time to direct our concerns to God and to our spouses or life partners.

Telling

The process of telling can best be understood as an attempt to work out an ethical sequence that denotes our understanding of who deserves to know. Obviously, we should tell those who most deserve to know first. But then it's a question of balancing the people who should know with those we really want to tell. Because timing and confidentiality are crucial, we should plan to announce our departure after an offer has been verified, usually the Sunday after our candidate sermon.

This sequence needs to be tightly orchestrated. Until now, we have probably kept the search, including all its ups and downs, from our children. They may have figured out that something was going on, but now it's time to let them in on the surprise. Because they are our children, they deserve to be the first to know. Because they are children, we don't want to let them know too long before we tell leaders in our current congregations. Telling our children on the Saturday after our candidate sermon and then spending the day together to work through the initial flood of feelings is a good plan.

That leaves the Sunday after our candidate sermon to begin telling the congregation and people with whom we've worked in our ministries. A special meeting of the diaconate or church council convened immediately before worship allows us to tell church leaders first, and to tell them face-to-face. It also may be possible to ask staff members to come in early on Sunday morning (prior to the meeting with church leaders).[9] Then we can announce the new call to the congregation during or after the Sunday morning service. Such an approach allows us to communicate our news face-to-face, first to our colleagues, then to church leaders and staff, and immediately thereafter to the remaining members of the congregation. Such an approach is intimate, and it may ease some of the bad feelings built up over the previous few months of deceit.

Finally, a letter, which we have already prepared, should be mailed first-class to all congregation members and friends on Monday morning. This letter should offer an honest and clear explanation of why we are leaving, give a brief indication of where we are going, and begin the process of saying good-bye. Many ministers add a personal sentiment, for example, writing that it will not be possible to say or do everything they would have hoped before they go.

Saying Good-Bye

Once the announcement is made, there will be a lot of questions. One of the most difficult questions to answer will be a simple one: "Why are you leaving?"[10] The hope is that the time we have spent in prayer and reflection since this specific call was extended to us will serve us well in forming our response to that question.

As Ed White points out, saying good-bye is a process, one that is not necessarily accomplished by making an announcement. Many of us will want to compress this part of the process. After all, it is painful. People we love are left questioning how well they ever knew us. And many of us manifest dysfunctional behavior that is out of character. It's easy to say something that will arouse strong negative feelings. This is a time when both congregation and minister go through the stages so familiar to those who work in hospice: denial, anger, bargaining, resignation, and acceptance. A death, of sorts, is occurring. No matter how mixed up the feelings may be on either side, this process deserves to be treated with the same respect we would accord any death.

For Your Reflection

- Recall people whose ability to wait made a lasting impression on you. Try to recall their circumstances, and what enabled them to wait gracefully. What can you learn from them?

- While in the waiting period, as you continue to pour energy into doing your job in your current congregation, pay particular attention to those ways in which your leadership can enhance the capacity of your lay leaders to minister. This may be emotionally difficult. Because you may be feeling unable to control your future destiny, you may have an increased need to control your current setting. Instead, let go and empower others. This will make the eventual transition much easier for you and for your current congregation.

- When you are confident that an offer is imminent, take the time to write down the answers to these questions: In your current position, what have you struggled with most? Of these, which issues should you work on in the coming years? What are your concerns about this new position if it is offered to you? Are you insecure about any of the essential aspects of the position?

  Review your responses to the questions above. On a third page, make notes about how you might use this new position, if offered, to improve upon those areas in which you are weak. Note any substantial gaps between the needs of the new congregation and your gifts. You may need to have further conversations with the committee before accepting.

- If you have not already done so, take a look at your long-range calendar. Are you committed to events scheduled for after your departure? Before you are saddled with the rush of events associated with your announcement, develop a strategy for each event in which you have promised to participate. Such consideration takes time, and it is better to take the time while you are waiting than try to fit it in when you are deluged.

- Look over the section on "Telling." What can you do to assure that the way your children, your loved ones, and your current congregation find out about your decision is respectful and fair?

- Take some time to formulate a sincere, albeit brief, answer to the question "Why are you leaving?" Avoid the temptation to come up with different answers for different people. Honesty and consistency, which emerge from sincere self-knowledge, represent the best policy.

CHAPTER 9

The Call Between Calls

For the first time in months or perhaps years, we are not leading a double life. Everyone now knows what has been going on. Still, we continue to serve two masters whose needs are very different. On the one hand, our new congregations want to draw us into their decision making as well as their dilemmas. It is not unusual to have weekly conversations with two or more leaders in a new congregation. On the other hand, our current congregants are doing their best to contend with the news of our departure. Now, more than ever before, their need for a special form of ministry is pronounced.

A Specialized Ministry

The specialized skills needed at this time bear some similarity to the skills needed to deal simultaneously with our own grief and that of a parishioner. The difference, of course, is that we are the cause of that grief.

Rabbi Edwin Friedman offers some excellent suggestions about the leadership and ministry demanded at this time.[1]

- When people react to your decision to leave, respond, but don't react. The time for reacting is past. In a while you will be gone.
- Allow other people to react. They need to work through their feelings to get on with the future. If you are upset by others' reactions, try not to act on your feelings. You have had months to get used to the idea and to work through your feelings about leaving. Now you must give them a chance to do the same.

- You can be a part of the transition process, but don't become involved in the selection of your successor. Likewise, try to avoid becoming overly involved or invested in instructing the laity about how they can best carry on without you, or how they should proceed in initiating their own search process. The best way to provide input is in a structured, formal "exit interview," which can be helpful for you as well as lay leaders.

With everything else going on in our lives at this time of enormous change, it would be easy to carry on with our daily routines, to simply put one foot in front of the other each day until we pack our cars and drive away. But what we should try to do during this time of transition is take advantage of a rare opportunity to test and develop our spiritual and ethical maturity. Ministry to our current congregations (and to ourselves and our families) will likely be more difficult than it has ever been before. It is a chance to die a little death, yet live to praise God and minister again.[2] What follows explores some of these opportunities.

Staying Centered

The Lure of "So Much to Do"

Rule number one: You can't do it all!

Realizing that our days are now numbered, we must seek to accomplish what is appropriate for this special time in our ministries. One way we ministers run from the pain of saying good-bye is overscheduling ourselves. That way, there isn't time to contemplate our own pain, and there certainly isn't time to seek out others whose pain we either know or suspect.

This is not to suggest that we should be idle. The point is to recognize that the most common excuse ministers give for making a bad exit is that there simply was not enough time to do it right. As with all things in life, we are given just enough time to accomplish all we need to accomplish. But it is up to us to recognize that the time is limited. Thus, we must prioritize what really matters.

Maintaining Prayer Life

Rule number two: You can't do well at any of this without God.

Our relationship with God will see us through this transition. There are people on whom we have depended for years who will react to our departure so negatively that we will feel like lepers. Our family members may become moody. We may become, in an odd way, strangers to ourselves.

Amidst all of this fluctuation, however, we can always depend on God. The irony of our modern prayer lives is that just when we are most busy, when we have even less time than usual for prayer and reflection, that is when we most need prayer.

Identifying What Really Matters

Rule number three: Forget what is urgent; do only the important things.[3]

Through our relationship with God, amidst this hectic time of our lives, we will be encouraged again and again to recognize what really matters. Emotionally we may have already made a good bit of progress detaching ourselves from all that we love in our current settings. Now, other arenas may need our attention.

Of course, what really matters will vary from person to person. Following, however, are two areas that deserve discussion.

Settling Unfinished Business

Each of us has congregants with whom we have fought in one way or another over the years. Now is the time to do whatever we can to clear the air, to ask forgiveness, to offer forgiveness, to somehow repair the breach. Some of our parishioners may wonder, as Ed White suggests in his book *Saying Goodbye*,[4] whether our feelings about them may have contributed to our decision to leave. Be honest about this. If they were adversaries, now is the time to settle the dispute, to communicate how the relationship felt, and to find a way to work with them to acknowledge God's love. This is the only opportunity we will have to do this. If we don't "finish business," so to speak, it will remain forever unfinished.[5]

Saying "Thank You"

There will likely be many opportunities, both formal and semiformal, to express thanks to our congregations. We must take the time to say "thank you" to those individuals who have really mattered to us, especially the people who have lifted our spirits when we have been down, the people who have told us from time to time that they pray for us, the people who have taken risks in support of God's call. In and outside our congregations, we need to say "thank you."

Family

Rule number four: Pay lots of attention to your family.

During this time, our families are likely to be under more stress than we are.[6] The complexity of feelings surrounding such a life change can be enormous. We need to signal, again and again, that their feelings matter to us, and that no matter how caught up we may be in trying to do right by our current congregations, we will drop everything to pay attention to their needs.

Being married to a minister is, in many ways, a huge rip-off. If our situation has been positive and we give it up, we leave our spouses and children with very little to celebrate. What may be an adventure for us is for them a forced evacuation. While we cannot control their emotional responses, we can communicate to them in every way possible that we care and that their feelings are important.

Grace

> *Grace strikes us when we are in great pain and restlessness. It strikes us when we walk through the dark valley of a meaningless and empty life. It strikes us when we feel our separation is deeper than usual. . . . Sometimes at that moment a wave of light breaks into our darkness, and it is as though a voice were saying: "You are accepted. You are accepted, accepted by that which is greater than you, and the name of which you do not know."*
>
> Paul Tillich, *The Shaking of the Foundations*[7]

Accepting Praise, Gratitude, and Love

Many ministers find it difficult to accept praise, gratitude, or love from their congregants. While a psychological assessment of the numerous possible causes of this is beyond the scope of this work, I must at least state that accommodating this reality is essential for a healthy departure. Whatever our relationships with our current congregations have been, many parishioners will want to express these positive feelings. Taking the time to listen to them is an important part of ministry during this in-between period.

Beyond taking the time lies the roadblock of opening our souls. Even though we have just "landed" a new job and should be "on top of the world," this time of transition brings on feelings of insecurity. We may be experiencing the equivalent of "buyer's remorse."[8] Doubt and uncertainty about the advisability of our decision to leave can dampen our enthusiasm. These feelings can become especially acute when we weigh the prospects of facing the unknown against the outpouring of love, gratitude, and praise we're receiving from the people with whom we have lived and to whom we have ministered for years.

We need God's presence in the form of grace to see us through these doubts and insecurities. Although these experiences are a completely normal reaction to a major life decision, they are powerful and complicated. Not only might we second-guess our own decision, we might second-guess God's role in our discernment as well. Because we implicate God in these doubts, only God's grace can calm us.

Dealing with Anger

Roy Oswald, in his classic book *Running Through the Thistles*,[9] suggests that two major areas are significantly affected by the way we deal with our departure, particularly the intense feelings of anger that some of our parishioners may express. The first has to do with the congregation we are leaving behind. If we deny and/or avoid the anger of our parishioners, these unresolved issues can saddle our successors with an almost insurmountable obstacle. Occasionally, even when there has been an interim pastor, the new pastor's tenure can be cut short because he or she becomes the focus of unresolved anger, frustration, hurt, and disappointment.

The other area affected by the way we deal with our departure is our own personal growth. If we duck the anger coming our way, or deny it, or passively listen to it without acknowledging our own feelings, we will likely find that we bring to our new settings the unfinished business of our old settings, business that can no longer be settled because we have left behind the people with whom we have issues.

The potential problems in both of these areas are powerful motivators for focusing our energies on the difficult task of dealing with anger. God's grace is essential to accomplish this. Our leaving is a death of sorts, reminiscent of the challenge associated with facing our own death. Whether letting go of our congregations or letting go of our current lives, we will most likely have to contend with anger. God's grace offers us a greater context that transforms the pain and disappointments to which we might otherwise cling. God's grace connects us with the assurance that all experience can be reconciled when it is submitted to God's care.

Accepting the Freedom of Grace

If we fail to be open to grace, our departure will surely be marked by unresolved pain, unfinished business, and incomplete good-byes. Even if we open ourselves to grace, there will still be pain, much that we leave unfinished, and many people with whom our conversations have been incomplete. But by grace, we are set free from this burden. Grace relieves us of the obligation to resolve every pain, finish all business, and complete each good-bye. In fact, both we and our congregants need God's grace, so that when the inevitable happens, understanding and forgiveness will prevail. In this is our freedom, a freedom that comes only from grace.

Legacy

Our influence on our congregations and our successors will be felt long after we leave. The decisions we make, what we attend to, and what we ignore in the final months and weeks of our ministries will shape that legacy. Our capacity to make thoughtful decisions is often diminished by the general chaos of departure, but we can correct this in part by making sure that we attend to certain tasks for which we alone are responsible, some of which are addressed below. Beyond accomplishing these tasks, however, we should also realize that our character is on the line. The concluding section addresses that concern.

Tasks

Wherever we have been, each of us leaves a trail. Even after ministering effectively to a congregation for many years, the trails we leave upon our departure may be poorly marked for our successors. Following are a number of tasks we can perform to ease the transition.[10] More often than not, time limitations will limit our ability to address all of these issues. Depending on the nature of the ministry, some will be more important than others.

First, however, a caution. Many would argue that congregations go overboard in asking an outgoing minister to prepare the way for a successor. While this is debatable from parish to parish, doing whatever we can to ease a successor's transition will not only help the congregation, it will enable us to leave our positions feeling good about our ministries, from beginning to end.

- Turn over all files to other staff and lay leaders, and explain any procedures they may be unaware of.
- State explicitly (either in a written agreement or in the official minutes of the governing group) the nature of any ongoing relationship with the congregation after departure. Clarity on this matter can save a successor a lot of worry when parishioners make inappropriate requests.
- Prepare a yearly task list or a calendar for the coming year. The successor can choose to change it as he or she sees fit.
- Provide the successor with orderly files, including the church's financial history and meeting minutes.
- Provide the successor with special instructions and information he or she may find useful, including parishioners needing special help and parishioners who can be counted on for special purposes.
- Provide the successor with up-to-date lists of the following:
  - Parishioners who are homebound and in nursing homes and the schedule of visitation
  - Current office holders and committee members
  - The six most important successes and six greatest defeats during the ministry

- Active and inactive membership
- Neighborhood pastors and clergy associations
- All special funds with an explanation of their uses

These suggestions might bring to mind other possibilities. Be cautious, however, not to leave a legacy that attempts to influence or control too much. For example, leaving an updated job description of each employee is important. Attaching notes about each employee's work habits, however, would be a bad idea.

Character

It often takes years before we ministers can be confident that we have established a good reputation among our congregants. Even then, lingering inaccurate first impressions often take longer to correct. Because one's character continually evolves, a congregation is always a step behind in recognizing and experiencing those aspects of a minister's character which are actively developing.

Our decision to leave may cause some congregants to lose respect for us. For reasons that usually revolve around trust, these congregants will feel betrayed. They may even try to convince others that this betrayal was one in a long series of untrustworthy actions.

While such activity can originate with conspirators, it is not always so. Our decision to leave does, in fact, go against values most ministers teach and hold dear, values centering on the connection between commitment and continuity. Therefore, our decision to leave is, in a sense, "out of character."

In this way, one of the most common metaphors describing the relationship between a minister and his or her congregation—that the relationship is like a marriage—doesn't work. When we marry, we commit "until death do us part." That is not true with ministry. But the fact that it is not true should in no way diminish the power of the commitment we do make to one another.

If we are to ensure that our reputations remain intact in the minds of our congregants, we will have to convince many of them that the values which we have taught and modeled throughout our ministries are embodied in this decision. Of course, how we communicate that point will vary from setting to setting and from minister to minister. What we all must recognize and accept is that it is incumbent upon us to communicate, again and again, why we are leaving for a new call. As is the case for all leaders, our ability to convince others will hinge on the extent to which we, ourselves, are convinced of our own motivations and values.

For Your Reflection

- Review Rabbi Edwin Friedman's suggestions outlined in the section "A Specialized Ministry." As you consider the difficulty of executing these suggestions, consider seeking the help of a spiritual director, therapist, or supervisor throughout this process.
- If you do not already do so, be sure to set aside time for daily prayer. Centering yourself on God amidst this swirl of distraction is essential.
- Take the time to read Stephen Covey's description of distinguishing what is important from what is urgent.[11] Then, make a list of the people in your congregation and community with whom you have unfinished business. Try to chip away at this list and take the time to speak with each person. Do whatever you can to depart with a clear conscience.
- Schedule time to spend with your family during this time. Remember, they are making this life change with you. They need to know that you care about them, and they may need your help and support in working through their own feelings.
- Even if you are in the earliest stages of a search, review the list of tasks a departing minister should undertake to prepare the way for his or her successor. Many of these things can be accomplished simply by building a well-organized infrastructure. Consider changes you could make right now so that your current ministry will run more smoothly and will proceed smoothly if a transition occurs.

CHAPTER 10

"It Is I, Lord . . .": Now What?

Few of us recognize in advance how much energy is required to accept a new position and say good-bye to a church we have served. If we have reason to be excited about a new call, adrenaline may propel us through the move. But at some point, perhaps on the drive between our former congregations and our new congregations, we realize how alone we feel. Behind us lies familiar territory. Ahead of us lies an overwhelming feeling of dislocation.

A Dream

"I found myself in a friendly woods at night, sitting on a sled-like contraption. The contraption, which had a conveyer belt on its base, was capable of propelling itself, with me on board, at speeds that seemed dangerous. I was leaving a place I knew well. I was heading out to a place about which I knew nothing. All I knew was that I had been given the courage and had been endowed with the skill to maneuver this contraption through a dark, unknown woods at an alarmingly fast speed. Although there was danger, I was not afraid. Nor was I excessively confident. I realized that I really could see nothing ahead, and that I could go over a cliff, or smash into a tree or a boulder, or fall victim to any number of fates. I knew that riding the contraption actually increased the likelihood that I might die, or at least be injured, but I sensed that all was well, and that this journey was exactly what God wanted me to be doing. Just before I awoke, I took off, whizzing through the forest."

A minister who had been at a new and challenging church for a year and half told me this dream a while back. He said he was finally getting a handle on the various challenges of his new position and coming to know the key players. He had been struggling to get ahead of the curve, to avoid being ambushed, to gain a sense of mastery. He had traded the spiritual disciplines he had regularly engaged in at various points of his life for long hours of work each week. Still, the Holy Spirit had shown itself to him in countless ways, mostly through the intensity of the struggles he had faced.

Together we interpreted the dream. The woods seemed to be the unknown journey on which God is our guide. The minister was leaving the place of familiarity and control, but not without a spiritual endowment in the form of skills to guide the contraption. The contraption itself seemed to represent the Holy Spirit, which cannot be confined to the places we choose but leads us to new places where there is no assurance of a particular or positive outcome.

The minister who had the dream later developed some doubts about whether his current call was appropriate for him. These were painful thoughts because, during the first eighteen months, he and his family had poured out an enormous amount of energy to make the present situation work. Although it involved great danger over which he had no control, the dream had a calm feeling to it. It reminded him that God had given him marvelous gifts, gifts he could draw upon to cooperate with the Holy Spirit. The dream showed him that his current endeavor would be characterized not by control but by adventure, courage, and discovery.

All That Glitters Is Not Gold

Even before we open the doors to our new offices, new congregants may have given us long letters detailing ongoing disputes. True, we are asked to assume the station of "spiritual guide" immediately, but at this point, we may not yet know where to buy milk for our morning coffee. Everything is new here, including the people.

In our old positions, we did a great job ministering to the people we knew, in a setting where people knew us. But here, we know no one. Not only do they not know us, many of them do not trust us. As we unpack, we begin to fathom what we have left behind.

Finally, with our heads swirling and having no place that really feels like "home," we venture to take a few risks. At a committee meeting, or a home gathering, or from the pulpit, or at a luncheon, we offer a few unguarded, unfiltered comments, only to realize that we have just walked onto a minefield without a metal detector.

In such a situation we would do well to remember that there are reasons for every transition, including the departure of our predecessors. Some of these reasons may be revealed during the interview, but rarely is a courtship process so thorough that it reveals all the significant pitfalls that await a new minister. The ministers who preceded us left for a reason, perhaps many reasons. More often than not, it would be naive to accept the "official" explanation as the only explanation for their leaving. It would also be a mistake to assume that the congregation at large is privy to the real reason.

The Changing Experience of Intimacy, Authority, and History

From time to time, we ministers forget that we are itinerants. At our current or former congregations, we may have acted as if our ministries there would last forever. That may have been appropriate, given the rewards of doing so:

- Over time, we have become intimate, accepting, and vulnerable with our congregation members.
- Our ministerial authority has become well established.
- As our ministry has unfolded, we have developed a shared history with the people of our congregations.

When we leave our congregations, however, we exchange that well-known realm for a strange and uncharted region. And, from the day we arrive, we will bear some responsibility at our new congregations. That's when the contrast with our previous circumstances will become painfully evident:

- Few, if any, congregants will know us, and everyone will be adjusting to having a minister they don't know.
- While a few parishioners may grant us some authority simply because we are ordained and have been called as their ministers, and a few others may grant us some authority out of respect for and trust in the

search committee and its process, in the minds of most we will have no
authority whatsoever.

- We will share no history with the members of our new congregations.

The following true stories focus on the arenas of intimacy, authority,
and shared history.[1] They illustrate how difficult it is for newly arrived ministers to break into a new congregation, particularly because the initial relationship with a new congregation is so dramatically different from what it
had been with a former congregation.

Exodus

Tim had just accepted a call as senior minister in a large church. The staff
included two ordained associates. Both had been hired by the interim senior
minister during the previous year because within nine months after the former
senior minister resigned, one associate retired and the other left to pursue a
Ph.D. When Tim was interviewing for this position, no one on the search
committee had indicated that this was unusual. In fact, they had provided
logical reasons for each minister's decision.

A month later, Tim planned to return to the congregation to visit and to
buy a house. Two days before his trip, the interim senior minister phoned to
let Tim know that one of the current associates was resigning. Tim met with
her during his visit, but she would not explain her decision.

Another month passed, and Tim again visited what would soon be his
new congregation. While there, the other associate pulled him aside, and
told him that he would also be resigning, effective the week before Tim
would begin. Once again, the associate would not volunteer the reasons for
his departure.

This forced Tim to develop a new set of priorities for his first two years
of ministry. The need to hire two associate ministers took precedence over
all other priorities, and before they could be hired, the routine work of being
the sole minister to a large church was overwhelming. As if that wasn't
enough, a week after he arrived, the office manager resigned because he
found Tim's computer expertise and high expectations intimidating. Neither
the former senior minister nor the interim had supervised the office staff
adequately.

The search committee shook their heads in disbelief, but showed their solidarity with Tim. They were as surprised as he was that such massive employee turnover, which eclipsed all other issues in the church, could occur. Fortunately, Tim had considerable experience hiring staff. Unfortunately, the task would so occupy his attention for the first eight months of his ministry that his long-range future would remain in doubt for more than a year thereafter.

Because Tim had come from a situation in which a high level of openness, trust, and friendship existed among him, his staff, and his parishioners, the realization that he was an outsider in his new church dawned on him slowly and painfully. The resigning associates felt they owed nothing to Tim. And while their resignations did not shock him, he was surprised by their unwillingness to explain their reasons. Tim had failed to anticipate the fact that what he considered "normal" communication could not be counted on. Whatever its potential may have been, the intimacy, the relational connection, was simply not there.

We must understand that when a congregation ends its interim period by voting to call a new minister, wheels that have been idle for a year or more begin to turn. When the ballots are cast, those who are "on the fence"— including both parishioners and staff—often make decisions based on first impressions or hearsay. Often, but not always, this is for the better. Those who are pushed by hearsay to the point of resigning may be better off serving God in another profession.

A Dream Come True?

Fred, a capable young minister, moved more than a thousand miles to accept a prestigious position in one of the largest churches in his denomination. Fred was concerned that there had been no interim minister at this church, but he was flattered that the selection process had moved so quickly. The now retired, former pastor decided to continue to play an active role in the congregation. This was a surprise to the young newcomer. After three years of struggle in this new setting, what had first appeared like a dream come true had become intolerable. Fortunately, Fred found another congregation where his ministry could flourish.

After his departure, the congregation secured an interim minister and hired a consulting firm specializing in interpersonal communication and conflict. The consultant attempted to explain to the church leadership the problem posed by the retired minister's ongoing presence, but her comments fell on deaf ears. Three weeks after he arrived, Fred's successor, Ted, invited the church leaders to gather to discuss the consultant's report. The next day, the retired minister told Ted that he would bring a multi-million-dollar law suit against the church for slander and defamation of character if that meeting was held. Ted did not convene the meeting.

Although it is unusual that new ministers will find their authority so severely tested so soon after arriving in a new setting, it is predictable that their authority will be tested at some level early on in their ministries. As new ministers, we must quickly recognize that the authority we may have enjoyed in our previous congregations does not follow us to our new settings. We must work to establish authority in any new congregation. This takes time, because authority is rooted in relationship and trust. Many new ministers make the mistake of continuing to build the relationships begun with the search committee, but it is more important to broaden the base of authority, and as quickly as possible. That way, when our authority is tested, we will have some relationships and the beginning of some trust to see us through.

An Encounter with Deception[2]

Four years ago, Jim came to his present church with his wife and baby son. Full of enthusiasm and love for God, the family was determined to make Jim's first senior pastorate a success. Then Jim discovered a few things:

- The previous pastor had not left for another call, as he had said. He had left because the elders discovered his adulterous relationship with a divorcée in the church.
- A mortgage payment of $11,000 was due in thirty days, or the church would lose its building.
- The previous pastor had convinced the congregation of 125 to take out a $500,000 mortgage on an old, single-story building in an undesirable part of town. Monthly payments: $5,000.
- The church had never been officially organized, so it was not tax-exempt.

- A balloon payment of $235,000 was due in two years, which no one on the board had known anything about.
- Real estate firms in the community wouldn't handle the church's property because it was considered unmarketable.

"The problems were monumental, all the more so because I had no inkling they existed," Jim said. "When we candidated, we stayed with the church chairman at his beautiful suburban home, complete with swimming pool. He never said a thing about financial problems. Everything looked solid to me. . . . I found myself facing more discouragement and depression than I ever thought possible. . . . I felt totally alone."

Jim was not fully, or fairly, apprized of critical realities that would demand his immediate attention. Whether or not he was intentionally deceived is unimportant. It should also be mentioned that some component of self-deception may have been at work here, since it is difficult to imagine a candidate failing to inquire about and follow up on so many of these issues.

The critical nature of these surprises brings into sharp focus the fact that no amount of sleuthing as a candidate will protect us from being surprised in a new setting. And that should remind us of an important feature of assessing and accepting a call: We must do everything we can to uncover as much as possible about the congregation to which we may be called. Nevertheless, we must always remember that a call can never be reduced to the sum of what we know about the job. As new ministers, we must turn to God when we encounter unexpected challenges—trusting that it was God who issued the call—and seek the resources necessary to respond with grace and effectiveness.

As funding for churches (and other non-profits) becomes more and more precarious, and as societal support for voluntary religious associations is less and less part of the fabric of our culture, savvy candidates will undertake an exhaustive examination of the financial health of the congregations they are considering before they commit. In the years ahead, the church will need more and more ministers who are capable of leading struggling congregations to financial health.

These and other stories reveal a shocking truth: sin abounds, even among Christians! We need to be conscious of the fact that, in changing positions, we are moving from the known to the unknown. Our lives, our reputations, our families and their futures—all of this is on the line when we drive up our new driveways. The risk, the exposure, is huge. That we will be surprised is a given. That we might be shaken to our roots would not be unusual.

So much of the context in which we have developed our relationships with God is now gone. Yet our survival—and furthermore our flourishing— demands an active relationship with God. We must pay attention to God in the first months of our new ministries, especially when we are caught off guard or intentionally undermined. A new church is a mission field. It may also appear to us to be a desert, a strange and lonely place. Only with great discipline and intention will we manage to stay connected to the spiritual resources our relationships to God make available.

Grief

It may seem odd to conclude this investigation with a reminder of the grief that will preoccupy much of our unconscious energy in the first few months of ministry. As much as some would like to think so, ministry can never be reduced to a bundle of talents invested in God's servants. Ministry occurs in relationship. It involves familiarity, vulnerability, and intimacy. While all of these were present at our former churches, we now find ourselves among strangers. They are full of hope, and so are we.

We may even feel "on top of the world" about our new calls. We may say so when friends ask how it's going. But we are also grieving what we have left behind. We need to face that we have moved—that we have ended our relationships with our former congregations—and grieve the loss we feel.

If bereavement literature is accurate, our culture is callous to grief, even over the loss of a loved one. How, then, can we expect understanding for a less obvious reason to grieve, in this case leaving one church for another? If we departed from our former congregations without facing our feelings, we will bring that "unfinished business" with us. Even if we dealt effectively with our departure, the depth of our love for and involvement with our former parishioners will likely produce an overwhelming sense of grief when we begin our work in our new congregations. Anticipating that our new congregants will likely be unaware of or confused by our grief, and recognizing that none of them knows us well, it is all the more likely that we will swallow our grief until it commands our attention.

Denial, anger, bargaining, resignation, and acceptance—these are the stages of grief. Before leaving our former congregations, we may have negotiated each of these stages. But it is unlikely that we worked completely through our grief. The process of grief is not linear; it is a spiral. It will be triggered again by the concrete realities of our new situation:

- We will find ourselves denying that we have done what we have done ("I can't believe I left!" or "I can't believe I accepted a call to a church that doesn't have . . .").
- We will become angry about the loss, the gap between what was and what is. Perhaps we will turn this anger inward, or direct it toward our spouses or new parishioners.
- We will bargain. We may begin to subscribe again to our denomination's monthly posting of employment opportunities. We may dispute our contracts with the moderator or president of the congregation. We may try to appeal to our alienated children by promising a vacation in our former communities.
- We will resign ourselves to the realities of our new situations. Amidst a growing awareness of their inherent challenges, rather than feel exhilarated, we will feel depressed, exhausted, or sad.
- Finally, we will accept that "that was then, this is now." Our vision will become less clouded and more clear. Our energy will return. New congregants will begin to draw out our gifts and depend upon our ministries. Trust will emerge. New relationships will develop. The pain, the hurt, the sorrow, and the loss of what mattered so much will fade, gradually giving way to a sense of gratitude for what was and gratitude for what is.

Having worked through a second round of grief so that we can accept with gratitude the irreversible decisions we have made, we are finally in a position where we are no longer "serving two masters," at least in one sense of the phrase. Our loyalty to our current parishioners is no longer divided. We are able to devote all our working attention to our new calls in our new settings. Any lingering concern about ambition, perhaps driven by disappointment that our new churches are not all we expected, will pale in comparison to the details of the new call.

For Your Reflection

- Consider ways you might investigate the history of a potential congregation. Two possibilities follow:

  1. Ask the search committee to provide a list of congregants who have recently experienced a crisis (such as a death in the family) or who may presently be in great need. Make it a priority to visit those people. It is best to get these names from the search committee (who may turn to other committees or boards in the church for help in putting the list together).

  If you assume a more reactive posture and simply respond to whomever asks for attention, much of your time will be taken by people who are nervous about the transition. Paying attention to those parishioners in crisis is a more effective use of your time: You will begin to establish history with each person. If there is not already a system to keep ongoing, confidential pastoral records, create one within a month of your arrival. Such a system will become increasingly important as you connect with more and more people.

  2. Schedule an opportunity to meet with some long-established fellowship groups in the church, or possibly some of the elders in the parish. Ask a lot of questions about the history of the congregation. Listen, but don't accept everything you hear as fact.

- If there are concerns about a former minister or an ordained member, pay special attention to these concerns by finding out more information from reliable sources. If you hear of none, ask around so that you're aware of what has gone on before your arrival.

- Within your first two weeks, meet with the formal leadership of the church—not the entire board, but the executive committee or the officers. Ask them to identify the "hot issues" in the congregation.

- Try to discern where the informal power centers are in your new congregation and develop a strategy to be in contact with these individuals or groups. Better to take the initiative than to allow passive-aggressive behavior to run its course.

- Meet with the treasurer of your new congregation. (This should be the second meeting with him or her, since you will have met once before you accepted the position.) In advance of the meeting, request as full a financial report as possible. Review the previous years' annual reports, too. Don't be shy about asking questions. One of the reasons for doing this is to communicate that you care about the finances and that you will give this area an appropriate amount of attention.

CHAPTER 11

Conclusion

Ministry is what happens when people discover the presence of God between them. Ministry grows as relationships deepen. As familiarity, intimacy, and trust increase, God becomes more visible, and God's direction becomes more compelling. Capable ministers strengthen this foundation in their initial years with a congregation by building trust. The result: minister and congregation serving God together over time.

When we consider moving from a church, for whatever reason, the foundation upon which we have built our ministries is jeopardized. While the business world accurately assumes that a newly hired staff member will someday likely move on, the church cannot. If ministers were to build such an assumption into their ministries, their relationships with parishioners would be stifled. As long as everyone maintains the unspoken assumption that a minister will be staying on, trust and intimacy can grow, thus providing a place of assurance from which God can challenge and stretch a congregation.

By initiating a search, we soon discover ourselves in the midst of an enormously complex spiritual and ethical landscape. Once there, how we make our ethical decisions will be tested and challenged over and over again. Some of us will look to principles or rules as we attempt to navigate this landscape. If we do, we will find ourselves trying to determine what is right or wrong as we face an onslaught of unpredictable choices. The examples in this book suggest the inadequacies of such an approach.

Recognizing that no hard and fast rules can guide us, I have offered few prescriptions. Instead, through a survey of the available written material and a review of numerous case studies, I have attempted to present a well-ordered tour of many of the more confounding dilemmas occasioned by a search. If, from the beginning, we recognize this entire endeavor as a spiritual quest and make use of the available tools of discernment, then the ethical conundrums that may follow will be far less onerous. By maintaining a persistent, prayerful openness to God throughout the process, we constantly update our understanding of why we're doing what we're doing. This allows us to respond with grace and confidence to the inevitable surprises and conflicts we will encounter.

In this way, spirituality and ethics are linked. The only way we can chart an effective path that responds both to the ongoing commitment to our current congregations and to our sense that God is calling us elsewhere is to consider God at every step in the process. Our relationships with God give life to all other relationships. The fruit of that spiritual exercise will be the grace and integrity we need to see us through whatever transition lies ahead.

A Better Way?
Thoughts for the Search
Committee

A sharp contrast exists between the search process a church under
takes for a new minister and the search process a company follows
for a new executive. The most glaring difference is the duration of
the search. Churches are accustomed to searches lasting anywhere from
nine months to two and a half years. Executive-level corporate searches
usually take from three to six months.

The primary goal of this appendix is to suggest ways in which the
search process can be accomplished more intentionally, more efficiently,
and in less time. Before detailing why this is so important, let me offer a
caveat: Briefer is not always better when it comes to a ministerial search.
In fact, the search process usually results in committee members developing new skills, new understandings of their churches, and new relationships
among themselves. They grow in these ways because the process asks so
much of them. Beyond the selection of the candidate, the process offers
enormous benefits to those who serve on a search committee.[1] These benefits, however, must be balanced against the frustrations that result when
the process drags on and on.

Often, members of search committees fail to anticipate what they are
getting into. Many are stunned to discover the intensity of the process, the
necessity for so many meetings, and the months—and sometimes years—
that pass before they are ready to make a decision. Because searching for
a new minister is a relatively infrequent endeavor, and because most search
committee members have no training in human resources, the members of
the search committee must ascend a rather steep learning curve.

While writing this book, I came across a professional executive headhunter who had recently served on the search committee for a senior
minister of a large U.C.C. church. Having also experienced some of the

frustrations so common among those who serve on clergy search committees, he was able to help me identify some modifications to the process.[2]

Charge Ahead with a Retreat

Whether elected or appointed, when a search committee gathers for the first time, members have no experience working as a group. Oftentimes many members know fewer than half the others. Such a committee can accomplish little until it begins to gel as a group.

Normally this occurs over the first few months of the committee's existence. If regular meetings are called, each gathering allows the committee to work together and build trust, which helps them overcome some of the initial hurdles of the process and is required in substantive decisions.

When I came to Cleveland, I was invited to be part of Leadership Cleveland, a civic organization for city leaders. Because the group accepts mostly CEOs in the application process, members made it absolutely clear that the applicant must be available for monthly meetings and the opening three-day retreat. They acknowledged that this was a big demand, but confidently asserted that it would be worth it.

The same could be done when a search committee is formed. Be frank with committee nominees. Tell them that the overall process will be incredibly intense, and that to be on the committee they will have to clear their calendars for a day-long retreat.

The point of a retreat is to build trust. Set the date of the retreat within a month of forming the committee. Hire a professional facilitator. Denominations could jointly employ these facilitators.

Seek Professional Help

The work of any search committee can be enormously enhanced by utilizing professionals trained in group facilitation. Typically, congregations have not gone this route for some of the following reasons:

- Professionals are outsiders and may not understand the unique needs of the congregation.
- Professionals are expensive.

- Committee members often think they have people in their congregations who are perfectly capable of overseeing the process.
- A professional might inhibit the committee's freedom or influence its decision.

While all of these concerns have merit, altogether they demonstrate what most search committees fail to understand as their core challenge: discernment. Few congregations practice discernment as an ongoing discipline. Thus, when a group of congregants are nominated to a search committee, not only must they get to know one another, they must also mutually acquire the spiritual skill of discerning God's will.

Professionals could assist the search committee in two rather disparate ways, each dependent upon how a committee engages the discernment process.

Hire a Professional Facilitator

If discernment is understood to require the full participation of the search committee at every stage of the search process, then a professional facilitator who is trained in group facilitation could be helpful. This facilitator would have to be sensitive to group dynamics and team building, of course. More specifically, however, he or she would have to be experienced in the activities and approaches groups utilize to discern God's will.[3] This would not be an abstract exercise. After agreeing on a common understanding of what it means to be led by the Holy Spirit through the entire process, the facilitator could work with the committee in every phase of the search to assure that the committee is actively engaged in discernment and not merely in decision making.

Hire a Clergy Placement Specialist

Although there are benefits for a committee to be fully engaged in every aspect of the search process, it may not be necessary. A review of the search process indicates that it can be broken down into a few distinct parts:

- Selection of the committee
- Clarification of the church's identity
- Development of the qualities the church is seeking in a new minister
- Recruitment of candidates
- Review of applications
- Decision making
- Promotion of candidate
- Support for the new minister

The start-up process for search committees takes so long, in part, because committee members typically have no experience searching for and evaluating qualified candidates for a job—in this case, a minister. Much of the first three months is spent getting familiar with the process.

If a successful conclusion of the process is a good match between clergy and congregation, what roles must the search committee play? Is whittling a stack of 60 applications down to a group of 10 applications essential? Most committee members with whom I have spoken would regard that task as onerous, but nevertheless good practice for evaluating final candidates. But is it essential to the discernment process that the committee of lay people develop a short-term expertise in the area of reviewing profiles?

What if a number of professional search firms with the expertise to assist search committees were to sprout up across the country? The role of such a firm could be as follows:

- To establish a relationship with the committee and act on behalf of the church's mission as dictated by the committee.
- To utilize denominational resources and other networks to advertise the position and quickly identify a pool of candidates.
- To provide someone on the committee, if desired, access to all the profiles so that at least one member of the committee could assure that no candidate of interest was passed over.
- To screen the pool of candidates and present a small group of qualified ministers to the committee. For this task, the firm would use a variety of methods, including questionnaires specific to the congregation, review of audio and video tapes, telephone interviews, telephone references, Internet teleconferencing, on-site visits, and so on.

This could be expensive. A large church looking for a senior minister could see a bill of $30,000, plus expenses. But when you examine the tangible and intangible opportunity costs borne by a congregation in transition between ministers, that same large church is looking at a process that could span one or two years. During that time, stewardship among the faithful is likely to flag, and members who are on the periphery are likely to drift elsewhere. If spending $30,000 could accelerate the process by even six months, a large church could readily justify such an expenditure.

I would emphasize that this would not be the work of just any headhunter. I would imagine that a firm specializing in executive searches for non-profits would be the best fit.

Require Up-to-Date Profiles

Another frustration search committees encounter is that clergy often circulate out-of-date profiles. In the business world, it is unimaginable that a job candidate would fail to provide a current resume. The same expectations are appropriate in the clergy world.

Denominational offices that serve as clearinghouses could mandate that no profile more than two years out-of-date be circulated. This would obligate clergy to pay more careful attention to this aspect of their professional representation. It would also be part of a strategy to reduce the awkwardness that arises when clergy update their profiles and ask current congregants to write references.

Encourage Newly Placed Clergy to Update Profile Immediately

At what point, after coming to a new church, is it wise for clergy to update their profiles? Unfortunately, if a minister does it in the first year or two of a new position, it is almost certain that eyebrows will be raised in fear that he or she is considering leaving.

Why not establish a denominational procedure that urges all clergy to update their profiles between nine months and one year after arriving at a new position? This would certainly allay much of the anxiety that arises within the congregation when a minister starts asking for references. Such a procedure could also be linked to establishing a regular evaluation process, an idea that has merit in its own right.

Denominations could encourage clergy to initiate an evaluation within the same time period, an evaluation they could attach to their profiles. Among the many benefits of this procedure: it would encourage clergy to take the initiative in their own evaluations; it would assure that a professional process of regular evaluation is engaged early in one's ministry; and, if timed to occur with the updating of one's profile, it would make for an efficient use of the minister's time, since the evaluation would address many of the same questions and issues involved in updating a profile.

Keep the Congregation's Mission Statement and Vision Up-to-Date

An effective search process requires that the committee be able to communicate accurately a sense of the congregation's identity, that is, its mission and its vision. If for any reason a church is unclear about its mission, or if it is significantly conflicted, or if the departure of its minister has led to a church's uncertainty about vision or mission, then the search process will have to wait until the church can agree. An outside facilitator who is trained in helping groups identify their core mission could help direct this process. Such work usually cannot be done effectively by an interim minister, simply because he or she has too much else to do.

When churches engage the process of developing an up-to-date profile, they frequently discover a good bit of underlying conflict in their congregation or a wide variation of the sense of the institution's purpose, or they find themselves surprised to learn something fundamental about the congregation (for example, that the average age of parishioners is 63, or that a sizable endowment is never reviewed at annual meetings). These discoveries are best made in the context of a mission review, which can then inform the development of a church profile.

Getting On with the Lord's Work

Because discernment and struggle go hand in hand, the search process will always be challenging. Nevertheless, some of the frustrations so common to searches can be eliminated. Adopting the changes presented in this appendix could substantially reduce the length of the time between settled ministers while still maintaining the authenticity of the discernment process. I suspect that in the years ahead, the average length of service by a minister to a particular congregation will continue to drop, not unlike what has been happening throughout the country in the secular job market. While many congregations want to accelerate the interim period for the wrong reasons—and interim ministers need to be direct and intentional about how long that period should be[4]—it is a mistake to prolong the interim period because the search process is needlessly cumbersome. Amidst the chaos most transition produces, we must remember that every congregation has a mission. Although the search process sometimes helps a congregation to refocus and re-evaluate that mission, it can also detract from it.

NOTES

Preface

1. Robert Schnase, *Ambition in Ministry: Our Spiritual Struggle with Success, Achievement and Competition* (Nashville: Abingdon Press, 1993), 10.

2. For a discussion on the benefits of ambition in ministry, see Schnase, *Ambition*, 10-15.

3. As an undergraduate at Princeton, I studied with Paul Ramsey and Gene Outka. At Yale Divinity School and Yale Graduate School, I studied again with Outka, as well as with Hans Frei and John E. Smith in the philosophy department. At Andover Newton Theological School, Jerry Handspicker was my advisor.

4. See especially H. Richard Niebuhr, *The Responsible Self: An Essay in Christian Moral Philosophy* (New York: Harper & Row, 1963). Also useful is his *The Meaning of Revelation* (New York: Macmillan, 1941), which examines how God is known and how human nature is known in the knowledge of God.

Introduction

1. Throughout this book, I will use the word profile as a generic reference. When it refers to materials circulated by the candidate, I will call it a "clergy profile." When it refers to materials circulated by the congregation, I will call it a "church profile."

2. For a useful summary of the methods of clergy placement in 19 of the largest Protestant denominations in the United States, see Christopher C. Moore, *Opening the Clergy Parachute: Soft Landings for Church Leaders Who Are Seeking a Change* (Nashville: Abingdon Press, 1995), app. A, 151-52.

3. The following denominations follow this method of placement: the American Baptist Churches in the U.S.A., the Christian Church (Disciples of Christ), the United Church of Christ, the Unitarian Universalist Association. Many of the situations evaluated in this book will also apply to the following denominations: Assemblies of God, Episcopal Church, Lutheran Church of America, Presbyterian Church (U.S.A.), Seventh-Day Adventist Church, Southern Baptist Convention.

4. In preparation for writing this book, I interviewed half a dozen clergy, received written responses to my interview questions from half a dozen other clergy, and spoke with over a dozen additional clergy on one or another specific aspect of the search process. Throughout the text, I will draw upon these conversations, some of which are presented as case studies.

Chapter 1

1. Bob Dylan, "Gotta Serve Somebody," on *Slow Train Comin'*, Columbia Records, 1979, 1986, CBS CK 36120.

2. Moore, *Opening the Clergy Parachute*, 16.

3. Loren B. Mead, *Critical Moment of Ministry: A Change of Pastors* (Washington, D.C.: The Alban Institute, 1986), 18.

4. Wm. Bud Phillips, *Pastoral Transitions: From Endings to New Beginnings* (Washington, D.C.: The Alban Institute, 1988), 1.

5. William Sloane Coffin Jr., *A Passion for the Possible: A Message to U.S. Churches* (Louisville: Westminster/John Knox Press, 1993), 75-83.

6. Coffin Jr., *Passion for the Possible*, 77-78.

7. As suggested by Schnase, *Ambition*, 97.

8. See again Gen. 22 in the context of the promise made in Gen. 17:17b, 19b.

9. Danny E. Morris and Charles M. Olsen, *Discerning God's Will Together: A Spiritual Practice for the Church* (Bethesda, Md.: The Alban Institute, 1997), 36-41.

Chapter 2

1. Moore, *Opening the Clergy Parachute*, and the first three essays in Richard Bolles, Russell C. Ayers, Arthur F. Miller, and Loren B. Mead, *Your Next Pastorate: Starting the Search* (Washington, D.C.: The Alban Institute, 1990), 1-64.

2. Jim Berkley and Marshall Shelléy, "The Pastor's Parachute," an

interview with Richard Nelson Bolles, *Leadership* 11, no. 3 (summer 1990): 20.

3. Ed Bratcher, Robert Kemper, and Douglas Scott, *Mastering Transitions* (Portland: Multnomah Press, 1991), 16-18.

4. Berkley and Shelley, "Pastor's Parachute," 23-24.

5. See Ben Patterson, "Is Ministry a Career?" *Leadership* 11, no. 3 (summer 1990), 54-55. While Patterson is unique in attempting to unpack the notion of God's call, he seems to be saying that God works only through what Patterson refers to as dramatic "untamed calls." I believe God also works within us and through our changing circumstances.

6. James D. Berkley identifies many of the ways ambition makes its presence known in ministers. He also argues that ambition rooted in Christ can be holy. See his "Holy Ambition or Wholly Ambitious?" *Leadership* 11, no. 3 (summer 1990), 28-35.

7. Parker J. Palmer, "Threatened with Resurrection: Acts of Death or New Life," in *The Active Life: Wisdom for Work, Creativity and Caring* (San Francisco: Jossey-Bass Publishers, 1991), 140.

8. Palmer, "Threatened with Resurrection," 140.

9. Palmer, "Threatened with Resurrection," 141. Palmer notes that, although he has heard this story from several people, he has never seen this story in print and has no knowledge of its origin.

10. Bolles, Ayers, Miller, and Mead, *Your Next Pastorate*, 8-25.

Chapter 3

1. See Dean E. Foose, "Looking for a New Pastor? Looking for a New Call?" *Congregations* 23, no. 3 (May/June 1996): 8.

2. See James Hillman, *The Soul's Code: In Search of Character and Calling* (New York: Random House, 1996), 256. This probing work offers much of benefit to any candidate in search of a new position.

3. Berkley and Shelley, "Pastor's Parachute," 19.

4. It must also be said that new initiatives by the minister are not always in the best interest of or responsive to the deepest needs of the congregation. This is a crucial and delicate matter of discernment.

5. T. S. Eliot, "Little Gidding," *Four Quartets*, in *Norton Anthology of Modern Poetry*, 2d ed., ed. Richard Ellmann and Robert O'Clair (New York: W.W. Norton & Co., 1973), 510.

6. Bolles, Ayers, Miller, and Mead, *Your Next Pastorate*, 79.

7. William Bridges, *Transitions: Making Sense of Life's Changes* (Reading: Addison-Wesley, 1980).

8. See Phillips, *Pastoral Transitions*, 2-24.

Chapter 4

1. It must be said that on rare occasion ministers do tell their congregations (more commonly a few leaders in their congregation) that they are initiating a search that may take them to another church. I have seen this happen in circumstances where the minister is severely underpaid and the congregation is grateful for the period of service. It also happens with more frequency among associates for whom "moving on" is virtually a foregone conclusion.

2. United Church of Christ, Office for Church Life and Leadership, *Book of Worship, United Church of Christ* (New York: United Church of Christ Office for Church Life and Leadership, 1986), 407.

3. Sissela Bok, *Lying: Moral Choice in Public and Private Life* (New York: Vintage Books, 1989), 176.

4. Bok, *Lying*, 176.

5. Bok, *Lying*, 177-78.

6. See the appendix, "A Better Way?" which suggests as normal protocol that newly placed clergy update their profiles immediately upon arriving at a new church. If the initiative for this came from the middle judicatory, the minister would be relieved of the responsibility to take the initiative.

7. For some additional thoughts on what to say to potential references, see Moore, *Opening the Clergy Parachute*, 47-48.

Chapter 5

1. Bolles, Ayers, Miller, and Mead, *Your Next Pastorate*, 35.

2. For a refreshing story of a minister who, with his wife, sought the council of their ongoing support group, see Bratcher, Kemper, and Scott, *Mastering Transitions*, 15-16.

3. See Bolles, Ayers, Miller, and Mead, *Your Next Pastorate*, 36.

4. Calvin C. Ratz's essay "The Loneliest Choice of All" makes this point in both content and title. See Paul D. Robbins, ed., *When It's Time to Move: A Guide to Changing Churches* (Carol Stream, Ill.: Christianity Today, Inc.; Waco, Texas: Word Books, 1985), 11-24.

5. In Edward A. White, *Saying Goodbye: A Time of Growth for Congregations and Pastors* (Washington, D.C.: The Alban Institute, 1990), 23-42.

6. Although his discussion about our need to talk with others as we

approach a search for a new position is helpful, Ayers fails to mention the possibility or importance of talking with a spouse. See Bolles, Ayers, Miller, and Mead, *Your Next Pastorate*, 35-36.

7. Warner White's "Letter from One Priest to Another" is a thoughtful illustration of the value of long-term friendships with colleagues. His suggestions are particularly helpful for ministers experiencing conflict in their current settings and those contemplating a move. See White, *Saying Goodbye*, 3-13.

8. White offers an excellent list of seven destructive ways of dealing with the trauma created by transition from one parish to another. See White, *Saying Goodbye*, x-xi.

9. The Alban Institute has recently introduced a seminar entitled "Changing of the Guard—Making Pastoral Transitions." See also Bolles, Ayers, Miller, and Mead, *Your Next Pastorate*, 36.

10. See Moore, *Opening the Clergy Parachute*, 174-75, for a list of 12 centers.

Chapter 6

1. See Bratcher, Kemper, and Scott, *Mastering Transitions*, 20.

2. Emory Griffin, "Self-Disclosure: How Far to Go?" in Robbins, *When It's Time to Move*, 95.

3. Quoted in Robert W. Dingman, *In Search of a Leader: The Complete Search Committee Guidebook* (Westlake Village, Calif.: Lakeside Books, 1994), 71.

4. See Berkley and Shelley, "Pastor's Parachute," 22; see also Bolles, Ayers, Miller, and Mead, *Your Next Pastorate*, 2, 8-25.

5. See Moore, *Opening the Clergy Parachute*, 24, 29.

6. Robert Schuller is an obvious example of one such minister.

Chapter 7

1. Richard Nelson Bolles, *The 1995 What Color Is Your Parachute? A Practical Manual for Job-Hunters and Career-Changers* (Berkeley, Calif.: Ten Speed Press, 1995), 44.

2. A few excellent resources detail thoughtful, step-by-step suggestions to clergy. The most thorough and specific is Moore, *Opening the Clergy Parachute*. Also helpful are Doug Scott's "Getting the Real Story: A Guide to Candidating" and Ed Bratcher's "Coming to Terms," both found in Bratcher, Kemper, and Scott, Mastering Transitions. See also Berkley

and Shelley, "Pastor's Parachute," and for a thorough overview not specific to ministers, see Bolles, *What Color Is Your Parachute?*

3. See Moore, *Opening the Clergy Parachute*, 74-102; Bratcher, Kemper, and Scott, *Mastering Transitions*, 23-36; and Foose, "Looking for a New Pastor?" 9-12. For an excellent discussion of the interview process from the point of view of the search committee, see Dingman, *In Search of a Leader*, 115-50.

4. David Goetz, "Why Pastor Steve Loves His Job," *Christianity Today* (7 April 1997): 12.

5. This would suggest that we avoid leaving our children with their usual caregiver if he or she is a member of our current congregations.

6. See Foose, "Looking for a New Pastor?" 9. See also John C. Fletcher, *Religious Authenticity in the Clergy: Implications for Theological Education* (Washington, D.C.: The Alban Institute, 1975).

7. Dingman, *In Search of a Leader*, 121.

Chapter 8

1. Bolles, Ayers, Miller, and Mead, *Your Next Pastorate*, 70.

2. Bolles, Ayers, Miller, and Mead, *Your Next Pastorate*, 78-82.

3. I say "perhaps the first" exercise of ministerial authority because it is quite likely that, at some point in the interview, one or another opportunity arose to exercise ministerial authority.

4. Bratcher, Kemper, and Scott, *Mastering Transitions*, 35.

5. Bratcher, Kemper, and Scott, *Mastering Transitions*, 35-36; Moore, *Opening the Clergy Parachute*, 101-16.

6. This is a bit like what Werner Heisenberg discovered with subatomic particles: the process of observation actually changes that which is being observed. Thus, it is a mistake to attempt to distinguish God's plan from the observation of God's plan.

7. Berkley and Shelley, "Pastor's Parachute," 23.

8. Depending on the congregation, this may be a written agreement, signed by all parties and contingent upon the affirmative vote of the congregation. If we are expected to sign an agreement, elected representatives of the congregation should as well. This includes the president, or moderator, and the treasurer. The chair of the search committee is a good addition, but typically has no ongoing authority.

9. Unfortunately, staff who are not going to be present on Sunday morning will not hear until the next day. It might be good to honor them with a special phone call.

10. See Phillips, *Pastoral Transitions*, 25. The chapter entitled "Disengagement" offers both wisdom and advice about making "a good goodbye." Of particular value are summary affirmations a congregation can offer a departing minister.

Chapter 9

1. Edwin H. Friedman, *Generation to Generation* (New York: The Guilford Press, 1985).

2. Roy Oswald suggests that the way we terminate relationships with friends and parishioners when leaving a parish can be a precursor of the way we will face death. See White, *Saying Goodbye*, 109.

3. This distinction is profoundly drawn in Stephen R. Covey, A. Roger Merrill, and Rebecca R. Merrill, *First Things First* (New York: Fireside, 1994), 32-43.

4. White, *Saying Goodbye*, 110.

5. See Friedman, *Generation to Generation*, 258.

6. See Moore, *Opening the Clergy Parachute*, 120.

7. Paul Tillich, *The Shaking of the Foundations* (New York: Charles Scribner's Sons, 1948), 162.

8. Moore, *Opening the Clergy Parachute*, 117.

9. Roy Oswald, *Running Through the Thistles: Terminating a Ministerial Relationship with a Parish* (Washington, D.C.: The Alban Institute, 1978).

10. Many of these suggestions come from the following sources: Dingman, *In Search of a Leader*, 94-95; and White, *Saying Goodbye*, 109-14.

11. Covey, Merrill, and Merrill, *First Things First*, 32-43.

Chapter 10

1. Names have been changed to protect their privacy and that of their congregations.

2. From Robbins, *When It's Time to Move*, 7-8.

Appendix

1. Thanks to Prof. Jerry Handspicker, who made this point by quoting Margaret J. Wheatley and Myron Kellner-Rogers, *A Simpler Way* (San Francisco: Berrett-Koehler Publishers, 1996), 70: "People work on a small effort and discover new skills. Their energy and belief in themselves grow;

they take on another project, then another. Looking back, they see that they have created a larger system whose capacities were undreamed of when they first began."

2. Much of the thinking in this appendix emerged from a conversation with John Markt, member of Plymouth Church of Shaker Heights United Church of Christ and partner in Markt & Markworth in Cleveland, Ohio.

3. Examples of such activities are discussed in Morris and Olsen, *Discerning God's Will Together.*

4. The length of an interim period is a function of two distinct processes. The role of the interim minister is to assess the issues a congregation must address for the new minister to be effective. The role of the search committee is to engage a process of discerning whom God will recommend. There is no good reason to prolong discernment in the interest of congregational assessment. If the pace of the search committee ends up presenting a candidate before the interim minister has been able to raise and address all the important issues, however, the congregation is faced with a different kind of problem. If serious issues remain unaddressed within the governing board of the church, it might be possible to delay the starting date of the incoming minister. If that is impractical, the announcement of the starting date might precipitate resolution of some issues. It is also possible that unresolved issues will surface once the incoming minister arrives. No doubt, sensitivity to this possibility is needed, especially if search committees begin to accelerate their pace.

Achtemeier, Elizabeth. *So You're Looking for a New Preacher: A Guide for Pulpit Nominating Committees*. Grand Rapids, Mich.: Eerdmans Publishing Company, 1991.
    Achtemeier limits her analysis to helping search committees assess the preaching qualities of prospective candidates. A very helpful guide for looking carefully at this factor, which is considered most important by most churches.

Berkley, James D. "Holy Ambition or Wholly Ambitious?" *Leadership* 11, no. 3 (summer 1990): 28–35.

Berkley, James, and Marshall Shelley. "The Pastor's Parachute." An interview with Richard Nelson Bolles. *Leadership* 11, no. 3 (summer 1990): 16–25.

Bok, Sissela. *Lying: Moral Choice in Public and Private Life*. New York: Vintage Books, 1989.
    A well-organized marriage of ethical theory and concrete case studies, this book is widely recognized as the authoritative analysis of this topic.

———. *Secrets: On the Ethics of Concealment and Revelation*. New York: Pantheon Books, 1982.

Bolles, Richard Nelson. *The 1995 What Color Is Your Parachute? A Practical Manual for Job-Hunters & Career-Changers*. Berkeley, Calif.: Ten Speed Press, 1995.

————, Russell C. Ayers, Arthur F. Miller, and Loren B. Mead. *Your Next Pastorate: Starting the Search.* Washington, D.C.: The Alban Institute, 1990.
> A collection of essays for clergy as they begin a search. Recognizes the need for balance between seeing ministry as job, career, and vocation. Addresses special problems such as beginning a search while in serious trouble, advice for clergy with a disability, and dealing with delays along the way. Postscript offers a checklist for clergy considering a change and helpful psychological insights.

Bonhoeffer, Dietrich. "What Is Meant by 'Telling the Truth'?" In *Ethics.* Translated by Eberhard Bethge. New York: Macmillan, 1965.

Bratcher, Ed, Robert Kemper, and Douglas Scott. *Mastering Transitions.* Portland: Multnomah Press, 1991.
> An excellent collection of 12 essays covering various aspects of the search process.

Bridges, William. *Transitions: Making Sense of Life's Changes.* Reading: Addison-Wesley, 1980.

Chambers, Oswald. "How Conscious the Call?" *Leadership* 11, no. 3 (summer 1990): 59.

Coffin, William Sloane, Jr. "Career Versus Calling." In *A Passion for the Possible: A Message to U.S. Churches.* Louisville: Westminster/John Knox Press, 1993.
> Coffin offers a deft assessment of the distinction between career and vocation. His analysis of serving the higher good readily applies to ministry.

Covey, Stephen R. *The Seven Habits of Highly Effective People.* New York: Simon and Schuster, 1989.

————, A. Roger Merrill, and Rebecca R. Merrill. *First Things First.* New York: Fireside, 1994.

Crowell, Rodney J. "Spiritual Survival for a Forced Exit." *Leadership* 10, no. 1 (winter 1989): 26–30.
> One pastor's account of a mismatch and subsequent forced exit.

Crowell, Rodney J. *Musical Pulpits: Clergy and Laypersons Face the Issue of Forced Exits.* Grand Rapids, Mich.: Baker Book House, 1992. Although theologically conservative, this book is a helpful resource for both ministers and lay leaders. It also investigates the spiritual realm. See in particular chapter 5, "Survival Steps for Pastors and Churches."

Dingman, Robert W. *In Search of a Leader: The Complete Search Committee Guidebook.* Westlake Village, Calif.: Lakeside Books, 1994. Written by an executive recruiter, this step-by-step guide is a must-read for search committees.

Eliot, T. S. "Little Gidding," *Four Quartets.* In *Norton Anthology of Modern Poetry*, 2d ed. Edited by Richard Ellmann and Robert O'Clair. New York: W.W. Norton & Co., 1973.

Fletcher, John C. *Religious Authenticity in the Clergy:* Implications for Theological Education. Washington, D.C.: The Alban Institute, 1975. An insightful essay based on a case study of St. Mark's Episcopal Church, Washington, D.C., this book presents a theory of three stages of growth into religious authenticity: testing personal strength, sharing the search for professional authenticity with laity, and recognizing particular gifts and doing ministry.

Foose, Dean E. "Looking for a New Pastor? Looking for a New Call?" *Congregations* 23, no. 3 (May/June 1996): 8–12.

Friedman, Edwin H. *Generation to Generation.* New York: The Guilford Press, 1985.

Goetz, David. "Why Pastor Steve Loves His Job." *Christianity Today* (7 April 1997): 12.

Hahn, Celia A. *The Minister Is Leaving.* New York: The Seabury Press, 1974. A collection of 14 case studies of Episcopal congregations going through a change of minister.

Harris, John C. *The Minister Looks for a Job.* Washington, D.C.: The Alban Institute, 1977. A practical guide, targeting Episcopal clergy. Offers brief, helpful guidance on what to do and be aware of as one becomes more actively involved in initiating a search and finding a future direction.

Hauerwas, Stanley. *Character and the Christian Life: A Study in Theological Ethics.* San Antonio, Tex.: Trinity University Press, 1975.
Perhaps the best book-length exposition of Christian ethics understood as character. Hauerwas provides a useful basis for recognizing the connection between the method of search (agency) and one's fundamental convictions about the nature and significance of Christ.

Hillman, James. *The Soul's Code: In Search of Character and Calling.* New York: Random House, 1996.

Jenkins, Daniel. *The Protestant Ministry.* Garden City: Doubleday, 1958.
Jenkins, a congregational minister in London who teaches regularly at the University of Chicago, rewrote some lectures concerned with Protestant ministry, broadly understood. These constitute the first part of the book. The second part focuses on the inner life of a minister, examining vocation and the work to become a servant. The second part may be helpful in suggesting spiritual issues that ministers in search of a new call must examine.

Jinkins, Michael. "Re-Called by God." *Leadership* 11, no. 3 (summer 1990): 58–59.

Johnson, Emmett V. *Work of the Pastoral Relations Committee.* Valley Forge: Judson Press, 1983.
A former executive minister in the American Baptist Church offers a comprehensive guide for search committees.

Ketcham, Bunty. *So You're on the Search Committee.* Washington, D.C.: The Alban Institute, 1985.
An Alban Institute staff member interviews the author in this candid and concrete work. Ketcham is a consultant in organization development (focusing on transitions) and at the time of writing had recently served on three search committees.

Mead, Loren B. *Critical Moment of Ministry: A Change of Pastors.* Washington, D.C.: The Alban Institute, 1986.
A persistently positive assessment of the possibilities for exploration

and renewal amidst a pastoral transition. Organized chronologically by stages of transition, this book addresses issues from the perspectives of various participants in the process as they carry out their respective roles. Mead demonstrates a solid understanding of power dynamics.

————, Ruth Libbey, and Fred Wolf. *Choice Points*. Washington, D.C.: The Alban Institute, 1977; Reprint 1986.
A brief pamphlet for search committees.

Moore, Christopher C. *Opening the Clergy Parachute: Soft Landings for Church Leaders Who Are Seeking a Change*. Nashville: Abingdon Press, 1995.
A practical, step-by-step guide for clergy to begin and complete a search. Offers dozens of concrete exercises and suggestions that will help clergy to clarify their thinking and consider some of the larger questions.

Morris, Danny E., and Charles M. Olsen. *Discerning God's Will Together: A Spiritual Practice for the Church*. Bethesda, Md.: The Alban Institute, 1997.

Niebuhr, H. Richard. *The Responsible Self: An Essay in Christian Moral Philosophy*. New York: Harper & Row, 1963.
Niebuhr's theory of responsibility, centered in the relationship between initiator and interpreter, sheds light on the ethical dilemmas that arise in the search process. Niebuhr's concern with accountability and social solidarity broaden his understanding of responsibility to include the social context. Altogether, this is a most adequate theoretical structure to apply to the various stages of the search process.

————. *The Meaning of Revelation*. New York: Macmillan, 1941.

Newton, John. "How Do I Know I'm Called?" *Leadership* 11, no. 3 (summer 1990): 55–57.

Nouwen, Henri. "Finding Vocation in Downward Mobility." *Leadership* 11, no. 3 (summer 1990): 60–61.

Oswald, Roy M. *New Beginnings: Pastorate Start-up Workbook*. Washington, D.C.: The Alban Institute, 1977.

————. *The Pastor As Newcomer.* Washington, D.C.: The Alban Institute, 1977.
    Similar to *Running Through the Thistles,* this monograph draws lessons about beginning a new pastorate from Elizabeth Kübler-Ross and U.S. Army chaplains. The material on alternative leadership styles is especially helpful.

————. *Running Through the Thistles: Terminating a Ministerial Relationship with a Parish.* Washington, D.C.: The Alban Institute, 1978.
    This monograph is so good, it is disappointing to discover that it's only 19 pages. Draws insight from Elizabeth Kübler-Ross, as well as from journals and a study of U.S. Army chaplains. It emphasizes the positive impact of pastors who model termination in a healthy way and develops an understanding of death as the final stage of growth.

O'Toole, Patricia. *Corporate Messiah: The Hiring and Firing of Million-Dollar Managers.* New York: William Morrow and Co., 1984.
    O'Toole's case studies show that huge contracts used to lure corporate messiahs bring unrealistically high expectations that often lead to their dethronement. Pastors experience the same pitfalls, but without the perks.

Palmer, Parker J. "'Threatened with Resurrection': Acts of Death or New Life." In *The Active Life: Wisdom for Work, Creativity and Caring.* San Francisco: Jossey-Bass Publishers, 1991.
    Profound theological and psychological analysis of how we often prefer to maintain the status quo—even if it means death (spiritual or literal)—rather than take the risk of launching into something new.

Patterson, Ben. "Is Ministry a Career?" *Leadership* 11, no. 3 (summer 1990): 52–55.

Phillips, Wm. Bud. *Pastoral Transitions: From Endings to New Beginnings.* Washington, D.C.: The Alban Institute, 1988.
    Written from Phillips's experience as a Methodist consultant, this book is directed at both pastors and congregations. It speaks candidly about the more subtle and difficult issues associated with transition and offers valuable insight.

Robbins, Paul D., ed. *When It's Time to Move: A Guide to Changing Churches.* Carol Stream, Ill.: Christianity Today, Inc.; Waco, Texas: Word Books, 1985.

Schaller, Lyle E. "Succession, Transition, or Transformation?" *The Parish Paper* (November 1995).
A brief analysis of the realities of transition in church leadership, with a focus on growth, and helpful questions for pastors contemplating a move.

Schnase, Robert. *Ambition in Ministry: Our Spiritual Struggle with Success, Achievement, and Competition.* Nashville: Abingdon Press, 1993. Schnase offers a balanced assessment of the role ambition plays in ministry, examining its positive and negative influences. His enthusiasm causes him occasionally to lack objectivity in favor of an apologetic, but his many anecdotes are useful, and he presents many thoughtful points and questions.

Sidgwick, H. *The Methods of Ethics.* London: Macmillan, 1907.

Sonnenfeld, Jeffrey. *The Hero's Farewell: What Happens When CEOs Retire.* New York: Oxford Press, 1988.
Sonnenfeld's examination of the various "departure styles" of corporate leaders is very applicable to pastoral predecessors.

Stobaugh, James P. "Called by a Cry." *Leadership* 11, no. 3 (summer 1990): 57–58.

Tillich, Paul. *The Shaking of the Foundations.* New York: Charles Scribner's Sons, 1948.

United Church of Christ, Office for Church Life and Leadership. *Book of Worship, United Church of Christ.* New York: United Church of Christ Office for Church Life and Leadership, 1986.

Vonhof, John. *The Alban Guide to Managing the Pastoral Search Process.* Bethesda, Md.: The Alban Institute, 1999.

Wheatley, Margaret J., and Myron Kellner-Rogers. *A Simpler Way.* San Francisco: Berrett-Koehler Publishers, 1996.

White, Edward A. *Saying Goodbye: A Time of Growth for Congregations and Pastors*. Washington, D.C.: The Alban Institute, 1990.
White has collected and organized 20 reflection pieces, three of which are his. The essays range from psychological to practical, and include numerous anecdotes from the many authors. Of particular interest are the essays on the ethics of the relationship after a pastor has announced his or her departure.